Reversing Misinformation

How to Help Your Family, Friends & Community

Michael D. Miller, MD

MDMiller Publishing

Copyright ©2024 by Michael D. Miller
All rights reserved.
Reversing Misinformation: How to Help Your Family, Friends & Community
1st Edition December, 2024
Copyright of Back Cover Photograph Held by Michael D. Miller

No part of this book may be reproduced, stored in a retrieval system, or transmitted in any form or by any means, electronic, mechanical, photocopying, recording, scanning, or otherwise, without the prior written permission of the author, except for brief quotations embodied in critical articles or reviews. No part of this book may be used or reproduced in any manner for the purpose of creating or training any artificial intelligence technologies or systems without the express prior written permission of the author. This publication is designed to provide reasonably accurate information in regard to the subject matter covered. The author makes no representations or warranties, nor does the author assume any responsibility for errors, inaccuracies, omissions, or any other inconsistencies herein with respect to the accuracy or completeness of the contents of this book and specifically disclaim any implied warranties of merchantability or fitness for a particular purpose, and disclaim any and all liability arising directly or indirectly from the use of any information contained in this book. No warranty may be created or extended by sales representatives or written sales materials.

This publication is meant as a source of valuable information for the reader, however it is not meant as a replacement for direct expert assistance. **The advice and strategies contained herein may not be suitable for your situation. This book is not intended to serve as a substitute for professional medical, clinical or therapy advice. You should consult with a professional when appropriate.** The publisher and the author make no guarantees concerning the level of success you may experience by following the advice and strategies contained in this book, and you accept the risk that results will differ for each individual. Neither the publisher nor the author shall be liable for any loss of profit or any other commercial damages, including but not limited to special, incidental, consequential, personal, or other damages.

While the author has made every effort to provide accurate internet addresses at the time of publication, neither the publisher nor the author assumes responsibility for errors or changes that occur after publication. Further, the publisher nor author has any control over and does not assume responsibility for third party websites or their content.

Library of Congress Cataloging-in-Publication Control Number 2024923634
Author: Miller, Michael D.
MDMiller Publishing

Title: Reversing Misinformation: How to Help Your Family, Friends & Community
ISBN: 978-1-965581-00-1
1. SEL040000 SELF-HELP: Communication & Social Skills 2. FAM013000 FAMILY & RELATIONSHIPS: Conflict Resolution 3. SOC058000 SOCIAL SCIENCE: Conspiracy Theories
Non-Fiction / Self-Help / Communications / Misinformation / Health / Science / Vaccines / Climate Change

Table of Contents

Introduction	1
1. Understanding Misinformation & Misinformed People	5
2. How You Can Reverse Misinformation	17
3. Talking with Misinformed Strangers	53
4. Preventing & Reversing Misinformation in Communities	59
5. Election & Climate Change Misinformation	81
6. Social Media & Misinformation	101
7. Artificial Intelligence & Misinformation	117
A Few Final Words	129
Acknowledgements	131

INTRODUCTION

"Complaining about a problem without proposing a solution is called whining." [1]

This book is a practical guide to help you have productive conversations with your misinformed family, friends and co-workers – and people in your community. **It focuses on actions, not theoretical concepts,** so it's easy to read.

As we all know, during the COVID pandemic, misinformation became much, much worse. At least once a day I would hear about someone spouting misinformation about **vaccines, COVID, masks, or elections.** *That is an ongoing problem.*

I wrote this book because I couldn't find useful advice about how to have productive discussions with misinformed people. *This book is*

---

1. This quote is often attributed to Teddy Roosevelt, but it seems to be a distillation of his philosophy rather than something he said.
https://www.quora.com/Did-Theodore-Roosevelt-really-say-Complaining-about-a-problem-without-proposing-a-solution-is-called-whining

designed to be a solution.

The book's goals are to help you reduce friction in your relationships with misinformed people and loosen their grip on misinformation. With this book's guidance, you can help decrease the spread of misinformation, increase vaccination rates, improve public health, promote national security, enable more economic growth, and support actions to mitigate climate change. *You can make a difference.*

How to Have Good Discussions with Misinformed People

- **Don't correct someone's misinformation with facts.** That leads to a counterproductive "my facts v. your facts" argument, and hardens their belief in the misinformation

- **Do engage the person in conversations by asking them non-judgmental questions**, which will reveal:
  > Their reasons for mistrusting experts, science and mainstream media
  > Which individuals and organizations they trust, and why
  > The sources of their (mis)information
  > Their goals and motivations

• • •

This book is far from perfect. I wanted to complete it as soon as possible because public health threats will continue to emerge, new vaccines are on the horizon, natural disasters will devastate communities, and elections will take place in the U.S. and elsewhere.

I've included real-world vignettes and stories to illustrate key recommendations, and examples of phrases to use in conversations with your misinformed friends. To make this book easy to use, there are:

- Bullet lists of important points
- Bolded sentences and phrases highlighting key ideas
- Boxes containing specific insights
- Summaries at the end of each chapter
- Notes pages – after some chapters – to help you plan actions for reversing or preventing misinformation

Where I felt some readers might want deeper insights, I've provided footnotes. All the footnotes can also be found on the book's webpage: https://www.healthpolcom.com/reversing-misinformation-book-project-2024/, with clickable links where appropriate. (QR Code for that page is at end of the book.)

In no way is this book a comprehensive analysis or description of the problems of misinformation, or an exhaustive array of communications strategies and tactics. My goal was to make this book useful to every reader. I wanted it to be a foundation and framework all readers could use and build upon.

Since everyone's situation is different, this book's advice and insights are intended to serve as a guide rather than a strict recipe.

> **This book does not provide medical, other clinical, or therapy advice. I strongly urge everyone to have their own primary care clinician. If you need professional therapy for personal or interpersonal issues or situations, please seek that out.**

• • •

The book's seven chapters are conceptually organized into three parts:

1. Chapters 1-3 focus on one-on-one discussions with misinformed people you know – and strangers.

2. Chapters 4 and 5 focus on how to reverse misinformation through community-level activities, which could be local, state-wide, regional or national in scope.

3. Chapters 6 and 7 are about social media and artificial intelligence, which are significant forces driving the spread of misinformation.

• • •

I hope you find this book useful, and that it will give you confidence and some calmness in your interactions with misinformed people.

Because the ecosystem of misinformation is changing rapidly, I plan on updating and expanding this book in the near future. If you have suggestions for additions, improvements, deletions, or other changes – including your own success stories – please let me know via email at RevMisinfo@HealthPolCom.com.

And if you want to see updates about the book and other aspects of my work on misinformation and improving access and affordability for health innovations, please check, subscribe, or follow my website, blog, LinkedIn – and maybe even Instagram:

- https://www.healthpolcom.com/reversing-misinformation-book-project-2024/
- https://www.healthpolcom.com/
- https://www.healthpolcom.com/blog/
- https://www.linkedin.com/in/michael-miller-consulting2000/
- https://www.instagram.com/michaeldmiller2017/

Be Well,
Mike
p.s. The names of specific people in the book and in the acknowledgements have been changed, abbreviated, or removed to protect their privacy.

Chapter 1

Understanding Misinformation & Misinformed People

To cure an illness, you must understand it – otherwise, you're only treating the symptoms.

Arrrrrggghhhhh! That's the sound in my head when I hear someone spouting misinformation about vaccines, COVID-19, or other scientific topics.

If you've been in a situation where someone you know insists that something is true – and you know it isn't – this book is for you.

Chapter 1 is about why people believe misinformation, who is spreading misinformation, and why they're doing it. Chapter 2 is about how to talk productively with your misinformed friends, family and co-workers. (For brevity, I use the term "friends" to include family and co-workers.) The chapters that follow discuss how you can prevent and reverse the harmful effects of misinformation in your community – not only misinformation about vaccines and health topics, but also about elections and climate change.

• • •

Sometimes people will believe something that is factually incorrect, like the assertion that vaccines cause autism or infertility.[1] That is called **misinformation**. If misinformation is being purposefully spread by people for political or financial reasons, it may be called **disinformation**. For the sake of simplicity, I refer to it all as misinformation.

If you've had conversations with friends who've been misinformed about vaccines, COVID, or other scientific issues, you are not alone. Two basic surveys I did in the summer of 2023 and early 2024 showed that while there have been fewer of those conversations since the end of the health emergency, they are still happening and people want to talk with their misinformed friends.

It is important to recognize that misinformation causes harm to individuals, families and society. Misinformation about COVID and vaccines has resulted in tens of thousands of people refusing vaccines and then getting ill and dying. It has left many more with disability from Long-COVID.[2] Those avoidable consequences of COVID have impaired economic growth by decreasing the labor pool.[3]

The landscape of misinformation has evolved dramatically with the COVID pandemic. Before COVID, only 1-3% of people in the

---

1. I prefer the terms correct and incorrect (rather than right and wrong) because misinformation is about fiction that is presented as facts. In contrast, the terms right and wrong can be used for moral beliefs and policy positions, such as "eating meat is wrong," and "taxing the rich is right."

2. Estimates are that millions of people in the U.S. have Long-COVID. https://www.cidrap.umn.edu/covid-19/new-studies-estimate-long-covid-rates-identify-risk-factors.

3. https://www.brookings.edu/articles/new-data-shows-long-covid-is-keeping-as-many-as-4-million-people-out-of-work/.

U.S. opposed vaccinations. During the pandemic, that percentage shot up to about 15%. And the types of people who believe misinformation about vaccines has shifted significantly. Vaccine skepticism used to be found mostly among suburban, upper-income parents who often felt that so-called "natural" immunity worked better than immunizations. Today, the misinformed span the demographic spectrum, including people in lower-income brackets and rural areas.

There are now also clear political divisions about vaccines. Before COVID, the likelihood that someone would get a flu vaccination was not associated with their political affiliation. That is no longer true. Recent polling by Gallup clearly demonstrates that party affiliation is an indicator of believing vaccines are more dangerous than the diseases they prevent, rather than realizing that vaccines are safe.[4]

Misinformation generally doesn't start from nothing. It almost always comes from either a nugget of truth, or something that sounds like the truth – which Stephen Colbert labelled "truthiness."[5]

A common "truth nugget" that has been spun into misinformation is that people often get a rise in body temperature after receiving a vaccine. This is the immune system's normal reaction as it is preparing to respond if it sees that disease in the future.

---

4. Gallup poll from August 2024 showed that only 26% of Republicans/Republican Leaners think it is Extremely Important to get children vaccinated, compared to 63% of Democrats/Democratic Leaners; and 31% of Republicans/Republican Leaners think "vaccines are more dangerous than the diseases they prevent," compared to 5% of Democrats/Democratic Leaners. Those differences did not exist in 2015. https://news.gallup.com/poll/648308/far-fewer-regard-childhood-vaccinations-important.aspx

5. Merriam Webster dictionary defines truthiness as "a truthful or seemingly truthful quality that is claimed for something, not because of supporting facts or evidence but because of a feeling that it is true or a desire for it to be true." https://www.merriam-webster.com/dictionary/truthiness. Truthiness was declared the word of the year in 2005 by the American Dialect Society and in 2006 by Merriam-Webster's dictionary https://www.merriam-webster.com/words-at-play/truthiness-meaning-word-origin https://www.americandialect.org/truthiness_voted_2005_word_of_the_year

- **Vaccines do not cause infertility.** The temperature elevation after a vaccination can temporarily make a woman's menstrual cycle a bit longer or heavier. This variation from a woman's normal cycle seems to be the basis for the misinformation that "vaccines cause infertility."

- **Vaccines do not give people the illnesses they prevent.** A normal rise in temperature after a vaccination can lead people to believe – incorrectly – that the vaccine gave them the disease it actually prevents. That is why some people will say, "The flu shot gave me the flu." Because it takes a few weeks after a vaccination for the immune system to develop significant protection, if someone contracts the infection before then, they may incorrectly conclude that the vaccine gave them the disease – or that the vaccine didn't work.

Vaccines' link to autism is another false assertion. The misinformation that vaccines cause autism is based on fraudulent data published by a British researcher decades ago. Even though the publications were retracted[6] and the alleged relationship between preservatives in the vaccines and autism was proved false, this misinformation persists. (After mercury-based preservatives were removed from vaccines, autism rates continued to increase slowly, likely because of our improved understanding of autism and the accuracy of diagnosis.[7])

All those misinformation tropes are clearly wrong. So why do people believe misinformation? And who is spreading misinformation and why?

---

6. http://www.cnn.com/2011/HEALTH/01/05/autism.vaccines/index.html

7. The documentary "Shot in the Arm" includes information about how that researcher was paid by lawyers to produce published studies that could be used as the basis for lawsuits on behalf of parents who believed their children were harmed by vaccines. https://shotinthearmmovie.com/ Also see https://pmc.ncbi.nlm.nih.gov/articles/PMC6181752/

Why Do People Believe Misinformation

Since you're reading this, you've probably heard one or more misinformed statements from someone you know – a friend, family member, co-worker, or a person in a social group you're connected with, like a sports league. And you've probably asked yourself, "Why do these people believe those things?"

There are two basic reasons why people are susceptible to believing misinformation: First, they have a **very strong sense of personal autonomy**: they believe that they should get to decide everything about their lives.[8] The second reason why people are susceptible to misinformation is that they **mistrust large organizations** like government, media, public health organizations, large corporations, biopharmaceutical companies, and hospitals. People inclined to distrust those institutions are also likely to mistrust government and corporate leaders, and scientific experts, such as those involved with climate change.

> **Rural Farmer's Belief in Ivermectin**
>
> In the fall of 2022, at an event in a rural town, I was talking with a farmer and not surprisingly, the conversation turned to the pandemic. He told me that one of the problems was the way the media was withholding information from people about how to treat or cure COVID. I asked him what he meant, and he said, "Ivermectin."

There are many reasons why people mistrust large organizations and experts. People's mistrust is often based on their experiences, or family

---

8. Autonomy is part of the culture and history of the United States, and can be traced to the idea that the King of England didn't have the right to tell the colonists what to do. This concept is part of our governments to this day. States and local governments are the primary decision-makers on local matters, with the Federal government taking a secondary role on many issues. In places that have Town Meetings, every voter has the opportunity to be heard, and to vote on matters such as the town's budget, zoning changes, and other matters.

or community history. For example, some Black Americans may mistrust the health care system and biopharmaceutical companies because of their own experience with systemic inequities in health care, or historical practices such as the Tuskegee syphilis "experiment." [9]

Spreaders of misinformation often package it with statements like, "you can't trust mainstream media," so you have to "do your own research."[10] That sounds "truthy," and it empowers people susceptible to believing misinformation to be skeptical of experts and reject what they say.

Some Mental Illnesses Involve Delusions

There are people who have a significant clinical mental illness that makes them unable to distinguish what is real from what is not real. In the United States, it is estimated that 1% of the population have schizophrenia, which can produce auditory and visual hallucinations as well as paranoia. People with schizophrenia who are not receiving adequate treatment may believe that the government or their family is controlling them, or wants to do them harm. **For those people, this book does not apply.** Schizophrenia and similar illnesses require specialized clinical interventions. Families can support those treatments, but they should be guided by clinicians who know their ill relative, not by what is in this book.

Misinformation may also appeal to people who are struggling with the complexities of modern life. It may be difficult for such people to accept that an invisible virus can cause a new devastating illness and upend the economy, or that a new vaccine can prevent illness and death. For them, it may be comforting to believe that COVID is a great conspiracy among

---

9. https://www.cdc.gov/tuskegee/about/index.html

10. Describing certain groups as untrustworthy is a feature of conspiracy theories. The terms "mainstream" and "experts" are often used by spreaders of conspiracy theories to imply that the "others" are part of a conspiracy and their information shouldn't be trusted.

the government, health care organizations, and traditional media.

People who believe misinformation may get a psychological boost by becoming a "member" of a cohort of like-minded people. Social media serve as a communal echo chamber where they can interact with people who have similar perspectives. (See Chapter 6 for more about social media and misinformation.)

Negative information on social media is estimated to spread up to seven times faster than correct information because it gets many more like and share from users. Social media can reinforce misinformation by leading users to sites that their social media "friends" likes and shares. Talk radio, podcasts and video "channels" can also reinforce people's adherence to misinformation by making them feel like they are part of group that supports each other's views.

Who is Spreading Misinformation and Why[11]

Making money and promoting civil unrest are the main reasons why people and organizations spread misinformation. Misinformation spreaders make money by selling books, videos or products. They can generate significant revenue from advertising on social media channels and other "shows" if they have hundreds of thousands (or millions) of followers and viewers. Spreaders of misinformation may also use traditional media platforms – TV, print press and talk radio – to expand their audience and advertising revenue. Some misinformation

---

11. This book does not specifically address conspiracy theories behind the spread of misinformation and disinformation. Conspiracies theories involve a narrative about powerful, hidden groups seeking to control or manipulate the general population, or to keep some significant "truth" hidden from the public. Conspiracies and misinformation intersect when conspiracy theorists justify their misinformation, as in "Mainstream media isn't telling people that Ivermectin cures COVID." While some efforts to reverse people's belief in conspiracies have been successful, it is unclear whether those efforts reduce people's belief in the misinformation itself. https://www.nytimes.com/2024/09/12/health/chatbot-debunk-conspiracy-theories.html Also, for most conspiracy theories to be true, a large number of people in different organizations would have to keep the "secret" over a long period of time, which is extremely unrealistic.

spreaders offer paid subscriptions or memberships that may include newsletters and other benefits that reinforce the misinformation.

Successful spreaders of misinformation are often charismatic individuals who deliver simple, catchy slogans and phrases. Experts and others who try to refute misinformation may be much less engaging and captivating, and misinformation is difficult to refute in real time because science and nuanced facts generally cannot be condensed to a catch-phrase or sound-bite.

Spreaders of misinformation will often energize their audiences by claiming that people's constitutional rights are being threatened, using phrases such as "They want to hide the truth," or the government wants to "shut us down."

Talk Radio Spins Proposed Legislation Into Misinformation

In early 2023 I was driving to a funeral and tuned into a radio talk show where the host was railing against proposed state legislation that would lower the age of consent for getting vaccinated to 12 years old. A key false message was that the bill would <u>require</u> kids to get vaccinated. The host repeated that falsehood many times while stating emphatically (and incorrectly) that no kid had ever died from COVID. The nugget of truth here was that a piece of legislation had been proposed. The radio host used that nugget to spawn the misinformation that "kids will be forced to be vaccinated" – and leveraged people's mistrust of the government to inflame listeners.

Some individuals and groups may spread misinformation not to make money, but to gain **geopolitical advantage**. For example, one country might support the spread of misinformation about vaccines or COVID in another country to increase civil unrest and mistrust in the government. Spreaders of misinformation may use state-sanctioned real and bot social media accounts to generate likes, positive comments, and re-posts until their misinformation goes "viral."

Individuals can also use misinformation for their own political advantage. A politician or political candidate might send out misinformation to garner favor with supporters who already believe it. (See Chapter 5 about election and political misinformation.)

Altruistic Spreaders

Altruistic spreaders are a more benign type of misinformation spreader – but they still can cause significant harm. They believe the misinformation is true, and think they are helping others by sharing those "truths." However, altruistic sharing of misinformation may be even more harmful since they are likely sharing it with people they know well, who trust them and will be more likely to accept the misinformation.

Altruistic spreaders may be the easiest people for you to reverse their grip on misinformation because they are likely your friend, family member or work colleague – otherwise they probably wouldn't be trying to help you by sharing their misinformation with you. While they may have some belief that the government or "big media" are hiding information, they do not have profit or geopolitical motives for spreading misinformation, so it may be easier to loosen their grip on the misinformation. Moving an altruistic spreader off their belief in misinformation should help them as individuals, and reduce the spread of misinformation and the harm it causes.

Fear of Needles

A fourth group of people who may cite misinformation as their reason for not getting vaccinated are those who are afraid of needles. This fear may be their way of expressing their autonomy – that they are in control of their body and what happens to it.[12]

Rather than admit their fear or anxiety – which could lead to arguments about whether injections hurt – they may find it easier to present misinformation to their friends and family, such as "I believe vaccines aren't safe."[13] With up to 20% of the U.S. population having some fear of needles – ranging from mild anxiety to a pathological phobia – a subset of them may believe and spread misinformation.

Summary & Conclusions

- **Misinformation starts with some nugget of data or truth.** Spreaders of misinformation take that nugget of truth and spin it into a narrative that susceptible people will believe and repeat.

- People are susceptible to believing misinformation when they have a **strong sense of personal autonomy** and a deep **mistrust of large organizations and authority figures.**

- The most active purveyors of misinformation do it to make money or gain geopolitical advantage, or both.

- Altruistic spreaders believe that the government, the media, biopharma companies, health care organizations, clinicians, and other experts are not telling us the truth, so they share misinformation because they believe they are helping others.

---

12. An acquaintance refused to get the initial COVID-19 vaccine because they are afraid of needles. They missed a significant family event because they were not vaccinated for COVID. Not long after that, they decided to get vaccinated so they could go back to school in person. People can overcome their fear of needles if the outcome is important enough to them.

13. A possible clue that someone has a fear of needles is if they state different misinformation at different times. For example, they may state that they are not getting vaccinated because they've heard vaccines cause fertility issues, but later say it is because they heard that vaccines cause heart problems. While it is possible that they are being hooked on serial pieces of misinformation, it is also possible that they don't have a firm belief in any one piece of misinformation and are just presenting what they've heard most recently so they don't have to admit their fear of needles.

∙ ∙ ∙

Terms & Q&A:

- **Why does this matter? Isn't the COVID-19 pandemic over?**

    ○ The SARS-CoV-2 virus will be with us for a long time as part of the landscape of respiratory viruses. Misinformation is an ongoing concern because it has made people opposed to all sorts of vaccines. It seems that more people are refusing to get their pets vaccinated.[14] This is a manifestation of the growing anti-science sentiment that Peter Hotez[15] and others have written about.

    ○ Misinformation has important implications for economic development and national security.

- **Equity & Inclusion:** The pandemic illuminated many aspects of structural inequity in the U.S. health care system and society. Some aspects of the response to the pandemic were not inclusive or ended up being inequitable. Some communities lacked access to vaccine sites, and some people faced technical hurdles when trying to make vaccination appointments.

- **Confirmation Bias**[16] is the psychological term used to describe how people only accept information that supports their existing perceptions or ideas. For misinformed people, this means that they believe what is consistent with their misinformation, and reject anything that is to the contrary. Giving them

---

14. "Nearly Half of Dog Owners Are Hesitant to Vaccinate Their Pets," August 31, 2023, https://www.bu.edu/sph/news/articles/2023/nearly-half-of-dog-owners-are-hesitant-to-vaccinate-their-pets/ and https://www.ncbi.nlm.nih.gov/pmc/articles/PMC7877678/

15. "The Deadly Rise of Anti-Science," September 2023 https://www.press.jhu.edu/books/title/33293/deadly-rise-anti-science

16. https://thedecisionlab.com/biases/confirmation-bias

accurate facts or information will not dislodge their grip on the misinformation.

- **Loss Aversion**[17] is a psychological term used to describe why people are more comfortable with avoiding losses than pursuing gains, by a ratio of about two to one. People fear losing what they have and what they believe. Misinformed people will resist admitting that their decision to believe misinformation was incorrect.

- **Cognitive Dissonance**[18] is what happens when someone is presented with information that is inconsistent with their beliefs. This creates internal turmoil. It is easier for people to justify their belief in misinformation so they can avoid the mental stress of figuring out what is true. For example, when presented with scientific information that vaccines are safe and helpful, skeptics may interpret that news as proof that biopharma companies are spreading lies to enrich themselves. To resolve this dissonance, people must be willing to accept new information that conflicts with their beliefs.

---

17. https://thedecisionlab.com/biases/loss-aversion
18. https://www.psychologytoday.com/us/basics/cognitive-dissonance

Chapter 2

How You Can Reverse Misinformation

"Change Happens at the Speed of Trust." [1]

When a friend says something you know is false, such as, "The COVID vaccines killed millions of people,"[2] your first instinct may be to explain why what they said is wrong or why their sources are unreliable. But correcting them in that way will only lead to a "my facts v. your facts" argument.

You can't have productive conversations with misinformed friends if your attitude is that they're "crazy." From their perspec-

---

1. This is one of my favorite sayings about how to achieve change. I've used it when discussing how changes in health care delivery or financing happen, or why they don't. I'm not sure where I first heard or read it, and the origins seem murky, but it might have been Steven Covey – or not: https://www.healthinnovationyh.org.uk/blog/change-happens-at-the-speed-of-trust/

2. This is what happened to a friend who told a group of people he knows well that he had to leave an event to get a COVID booster.

tive, you may be the one who is "crazy" for believing the government or traditional media, or trusting biopharma companies.[3]

Don't have arguments, or treat misinformed people as crazy. Instead, use this chapter's guidance to have productive conversations with the misinformed people in your life. They may be a family member, co-worker or friend. For brevity, I use "friends" to include all those people you know well.

Providing Correct Information Can Literally Backfire

Before the COVID pandemic, research showed that when clinicians gave their misinformed patients information about the safety of vaccines, the patients were sometimes *less* likely to vaccinate their child. This is called the "backfire effect."[4] It's as if an alarm bell is ringing in their head, and when they hear reasons why vaccines are safe, the bell rings even louder.

Your goals for having conversations with misinformed friends are to:

- Lower the friction in your relationships

- Reduce how much they spread misinformation

- Loosen their grip on misinformation so they will do things like getting vaccinated or wearing a mask

- Lead them to no longer believe the misinformation

---

3. See "Have You Met People? People are Complicated!" in this chapter's Appendix

4. "Vaccine Myth-Busting Can Backfire," The Atlantic, 2014, https://www.theatlantic.com/health/archive/2014/12/vaccine-myth-busting-can-backfire/383700/ "Countering antivaccination attitudes," PNAS 2015, https://www.pnas.org/doi/full/10.1073/pnas.1504019112, and "The limitations of the backfire effect," Research & Politics, 2017, https://journals.sagepub.com/doi/10.1177/2053168017716547

This chapter uses misinformation about vaccines and COVID to demonstrate how to have productive conversations with misinformed friends and reverse misinformation.

How to Have Productive Conversations with a Misinformed Friend

You want your discussions with a misinformed friend to be collaborative – like a dance, and not a fight. Having productive conversations involves listening, exploring their reasons for believing misinformation, focusing on their motivations, sharing insights, and ultimately having them become more aware of the hollowness of their misinformation.

This process is based on something called Motivational Interviewing, which some clinicians use with their patients. Having these motivationally-focused conversations gives clinicians insight into their patients' sense of autonomy and what fuels their mistrust. This process is not like flipping a switch (or giving an injection), because **change is hard** for people. It is a **journey down a path** that explores beliefs, goals, and motivations.

You can have these types of conversations, because your relationship makes you a potential **trusted messenger**.[5] These are key elements of motivation-focused conversations:

- **Listening** will help you understand what your friend mistrusts, where that mistrust comes from, and what sources of information they do trust. By listening – rather than telling them things – you will not be challenging their autonomy.

- **Asking non-judgmental questions** about their misinformation – and their sources for that misinformation – will **empower them** to explain **their reality** to you. You are **requesting**

---

5. Chapter 3 discusses ways to interact with misinformed strangers.

that they share their insights with you because they are the experts in their own reality.

- **Building on your shared history** and interests can help you understand what sources of information they trust.

- **Focusing your discussion on their goals and motivations** will help them explore the emotions that bind them to their misinformation, and the **consequences of their choices.**

- **To take your discussion to the next level** you can use the **Ask-Tell-Ask process**, which clinicians use to guide people toward better health by helping them explore their motivations and actions.

- **Bringing in a trusted ally,** to go beyond your one-on-one conversations, will reinforce and expand your discussions. The ally needs to be someone your friend also trusts – someone who will work with you in motivationally-focused discussions, and won't revert to a "correcting facts" mode.

The rest of this chapter explores each of those elements. It includes examples of non-judgmental questions, anecdotes, and two real-world vignettes to illustrate the process. At the end of the chapter, there is a worksheet to help you build a plan for structuring your discussions with your misinformed friends.

You Are a Trusted Messenger

You may not think of yourself as a trusted messenger, but the good news is that you are one. Your misinformed friends likely mistrust experts or authority figures. They don't know them, but they know you – whether it's because you're in the same family, you work together, or you socialize, play sports, or engage in other activities together. When you have motivationally-focused conversations, you'll be talking <u>with</u> them, rather than talking <u>at</u> them or challenging their autonomy and right to make their own choices – which is what they feel experts do.

> **Vaccine Opponents Have Lower Trust in Clinicians**
>
> A reputable December 2020 poll found that 85% of adults in the U.S. trust clinicians as a source of information about vaccines.[6] The other 15% – who don't trust clinicians as a source of vaccine information – likely overlaps significantly with the people who have been misinformed. Only 59% of the people who said they <u>wouldn't</u> get the new COVID vaccine also said they trusted clinicians as a source of information about vaccines. In comparison, 96% of people who wanted to get the vaccine as soon as possible said they trusted clinicians as a source of vaccine information.

<u>Listening is Key to Understanding</u>

The first step in understanding someone's mistrust is **listening without judgment**. Your misinformed friend is the expert about their own beliefs and truths. You are not, and you need to appreciate that before anything else. Otherwise, they may see you as challenging their autonomy.

Listening to your friend's world view will help you understand why they believe the misinformation, who they mistrust, and why.

You want your friend to feel that you've been listening, and they've been heard. That pairing is important enough to repeat: They need to feel like you've been listening, and they've been heard.

> **You're meeting your friend where they are – not dragging them towards you and your world view.**

For many misinformed people, this may be the first time that someone they know – who may not agree with their world view – has actively

---

6. https://www.kff.org/coronavirus-covid-19/report/kff-covid-19-vaccine-monitor-december-2020/

listened to them, and not tried to correct or coerce them. **Listening to your friend without judgment will help reduce the friction in your relationship.**

A person with a fear of needles could open up to you about their fear because they trust you, and you are listening and not judging them. They might then admit that they are repeating misinformation about vaccines because they worry that other people will judge them for being afraid, or try and convince or coerce them to get vaccinated.

> **Listening to Unvaccinated Employees of a Large Company**
>
> In the summer of 2021, I was asked to talk with several hundred unvaccinated employees of a large government contractor that was required to have all their employees immunized for COVID-19. The first time we did the live briefing, the company insisted on a webinar format where the only people on the screen were the president of the division, the head of human resources, the moderator (who was trusted by the employees), and me. This meant that none of the employees were seen or heard, and questions could only be submitted via the chat function.
>
> During our post-event debrief, I explained to the head of HR and the moderator that we needed to do a second session because the employees didn't feel like they were listened to. This is basically what I told them:
>
> You've got a group of employees who don't want to get vaccinated. They don't trust the vaccines. They don't <u>trust</u> the government, biopharma companies, the media, the company, or you – and they may even <u>hate</u> some or all of those organizations – including the company. And right now, their attitude is, *"I'm rather get fired or quit than get vaccinated."*

> Your goal is to get them vaccinated. It is <u>not</u> to turn them into vaccine promoters. You want to get them to a place where their attitude is, *"I hate/don't trust everyone, including the company.... But you listened to me. So while I still don't trust the vaccine or want to get it, I will get vaccinated rather than get fired or quit."* Remember, your goal is to get them vaccinated – so they don't quit or get fired.
>
> After the debrief, we did a second session using a format where the employees could turn on their cameras and directly ask their questions – and feel like they were literally seen and heard. I thanked them for their questions and could also ask them to expand on or clarify what they'd said. This made them feel – at a minimum – that they had been listened to, their views were important to the company, and they had been heard.

Asking Non-Judgmental Questions Leads to Productive Discussions

Asking your misinformed friends non-judgmental questions opens the door for you to explore their world view with them. Example of useful **open-ended non-judgmental questions** are "Can you help me understand that?" and "Can you tell me more about that?"

These types of questions will show that you are listening – and not judging or trying to correct them. Starting questions with the phrase "Can you..." is a subtle way of asking permission to continue, which puts your friend in the role of the expert who can explain things to you.

One trick I learned from Larry King, the renowned TV interviewer, is to ask questions that cannot be answered with a Yes or No. This gets people to talk more extensively. For example, starting a question with "Tell me about..." or "Help me understand..." requires your friend to explain how they see things. Conversely, don't start with "Do you think..." or "Don't you think..." as those questions can be answered with a yes or no and may be seen as confrontational. Open-ended questions allow you to "meet them where they are," rather than trying to drag them against their will to where you are.

With active listening you are showing respect for their autonomy and demonstrating that you are a trusted messenger.

Change is Hard for Everyone

Change is hard for everyone. It is **not as simple as flipping a switch** to turn a misinformed, vaccine-opposing person into accepting vaccines as safe and beneficial. Change takes time, and repetition helps.

Spreading your discussions out over time allows your misinformed friend to process what you've talked about. They can then enter your next conversation better prepared to consider alternatives.

> **Repetition is Useful When Presenting New Ideas**
>
> Marketing and psychology research indicates that it can take presenting someone with new information or perspectives **5 to 9 times** before they will begin to change their views. That is why it is easier to educate someone who is uninformed than change the views of someone who has been misinformed.

What you don't want is for your series of conversations to be seen by the other person as a competition. As your discussions progress over time, you don't want your friend to rebut what you'd previously talked about. If they do push back with new reasons why their misinformation is correct, you can expand the conversation by saying something like "I appreciate your taking the time to look into this more deeply. Can you tell me more about how you found that new information and how it changed what you think?" This should steer the conversation back toward their reasons for mistrust, and what information sources they trust.

The next time you talk you could say something like, "How did it make you feel to spend that time and find the additional information?" Or "Can you tell me what it was like searching for that new information?" You can then delve deeper by asking, "I often find it very frustrating not being able to find a consistent answer to some of these questions. Can we talk more about how you find new information from friends, the internet, TV, and other sources?"

After they describe how researching the information gave them new insights, you can ask them, "Tell me more about how the new information changed your views." Their response may help you better understand how additional information could lead them to change their mind. You may learn more about the information sources they trust – which individuals, social media channels, talk radio shows, podcasts, and traditional media outlets.

You may get pushback if your friend feels like you're trying to coerce them, or convince them that they're wrong and you're correct. They may feel like they're being pressured to change their mind. You could pause the conversation and reassure them by saying, **"I'm not trying to convince you. I'm trying to understand you."** You don't want to keep pushing because **trust is gained in drops but lost in buckets.** By reassuring them that you want to understand them you will have the opportunity to reestablish trust as you explore their world view in greater depth.

Remember, this process is like traveling a path, not just opening a door and walking through it.

And like walking a path, exploring side trails gives you different views. In your discussions, those side trails would be talking about topics like sports, TV shows, food, music, weather, or family. Talking about topics other than misinformation will help maintain your relationship with your friend, reduce friction, and strengthen your position as a trusted messenger.

• • •

When you're talking with a misinformed friend, you'll want to find the right moment to end each conversation. A good time to wrap up is when you think you've made progress, have maintained the goodwill and trust in your relationship, and not created too much cognitive dissonance if you've presented new information or perspectives. To foster a good transition you could say, "This has been great. I really appreciate that you've taken the time to share your views with me, and I look forward to talking more." You could then suggest another time to meet, or plan on including the misinformation topic in your conversation if you already have plans to talk or meet again.

Your Shared History Can Help Extend the Discussion in Productive Ways

As a trusted messenger you may already understand your friend's history, circumstances, and world view, including **their reasons for being mistrustful** of vaccines, science, or government actions, including elections. Their reasons could be discriminatory experiences with the health care system, a significant reaction someone had to a vaccine in the past, a personal or family experience, or a governmental or corporate bureaucracy that was opaque or unfair.

Your **shared history** can also help you ask effective non-judgmental questions. You can improve the conversation flow by referring to celebrities, local community personalities, or leaders they admire – a business owner, teacher, sports figure, bartender, or member of the clergy.

And if you don't know the historical or personal reasons for why your friend is susceptible to misinformation, frame your non-judgmental questions so they will explain it to you. You could start with "Can you tell me more about that?" rather than the more confrontational question "Where did you hear that?"

Discussing Goals and Motivations Is Productive

A major part of your conversations with misinformed friends should be their goals and motivations. Focusing on what they want to achieve in life will help them see how misinformation is limiting their life choices. Identifying and discussing that cognitive dissonance can lead them to **disconnecting from their misinformation**.

An **individual's motivations** relate to their goals for work and family, relationships with friends and family, and social responsibilities, such as being a patriotic citizen who wants a strong economy and nation.[7] Your friend may not realize that their misinformation about vaccines and public health conflicts with their desire for **strong national security and a robust economy,** because unhealthy people are not able to serve in the military and cannot be productive workers.[8] Long-COVID – which is also a target for misinformation – seems to be harming economic growth by reducing the size of the active workforce.[9]

Asking your friend about their goals and motivations also demonstrates that you care about them and have empathy for them and their situation. If their views are very different from those of the people they interact with – including family and friends – that **dissonance** can cause internal conflict and angst.

You are not trying to directly alter your friend's beliefs. Rather, you are **eliciting their feelings** so they can reveal the **emotions (like**

---

7. Many people opposed vaccines during the COVID-19 pandemic because they viewed the economic effects of the public health measures (such as closing schools and banning public gatherings) as far more harmful than the illness. This reinforced their mistrust of government and the health care system.

8. The ongoing obesity epidemic has been a challenge for military readiness because it has reduced the number of people able to serve.

9. Economic Effects of Long COVID Even Larger Than We Thought," December 13, 2022 - https://jheor.org/post/1746-economic-effects-of-long-covid-even-larger-than-we-thought. And "Long Covid risk has dropped over time but remains substantial, study shows," July 17, 2024 - https://www.cnn.com/2024/07/17/health/long-covid-risk/index.html

fears) that connect them to their misinformation.[10] Your goal for exploring emotions and motivations is to have them to recognize that dissonance, which may lead them to question their misinformation.

Questions that can help reveal your friend's goals and motivations include asking about trips they would like to take, or things they want to do with family, friends, or work colleagues – particularly if those activities involve interacting with individuals who might be COVID risk-averse,[11] or there are places they want to go that require vaccines or masks.[12] For example, as respiratory infections increased in the summer of 2024 some hospitals reinstated mask requirements for staff, patients, and visitors.[13] If your friend wants to visit relatives in a hospital or nursing home but refuses to wear a mask, that would create a conflict between their motivations and their misinformation.

For people with school-aged children, you could ask them about having their children attend school, attend birthday parties, or sleepovers with friends, since those activities may require the children to have received vaccinations for measles or other illnesses.

---

10. A friend whose career was spent providing therapy noted that this is similar to the saying "F* the facts, follow the feelings."

11. There are also other respiratory infections that people with health conditions or risk factors could (and should) be concerned about, including RSV, influenza, other viruses that cause the common cold, and of course various bacteria that can cause pneumonia etc.

12. With the end of the Federal Public Health Emergency on May 11, 2023, it is uncertain what sorts of vaccine and masking requirements will continue. Companies, organizations, and public venues may require vaccinations or masks. Some colleges and universities may require COVID or flu vaccinations since students are living together in dormitories, just as they may require meningitis vaccinations if there is an outbreak. And in some states, it is a requirement. https://www.cdc.gov/meningococcal/about/risk-community.html

13. "Baystate Health issues mask mandate as COVID-19 cases rise," WWLP, August 20, 2024, https://www.wwlp.com/news/local-news/hampden-county/baystate-health-issues-mask-mandate-as-covid-19-cases-rise/; " TCRHCC Reinstates Mask Mandate Amid Rising COVID-19 Cases," July 19, 2024, https://tchealth.org/tcrhcc-reinstates-mask-mandate-amid-rising-covid-19-cases/; and "California hospital returns to masking as COVID surges," The Mercury News, July 12, 2024, https://www.mercurynews.com/2024/07/12/county-increases-testing-ucsd-health-workers-return-to-masking-as-covid-surges/

To be effective, you need to have discussions in a non-judgmental, non-coercive way. An important part of meeting people where they are is **recognizing that they are fully capable of making their own choices**. You need to recognize their rights, and support – rather than challenge – their personal autonomy. Any appearance that you're challenging their right to make their own choices will undermine your status as a trusted messenger.

Statements that can help you emphasize their right to make their own choices are, "These are your choices for you to make." Or "You are in control of your life choices." And depending on the tenor of your discussion to this point, you can follow up with, "However, all choices have consequences – even choices not to make decisions, like not returning phone calls, not buying a lottery ticket, not exercising, or not to taking a job."

**Your goal is not to make choices for people.
Your goal is to help people make informed choices rather than misinformed ones.**

Society doesn't provide complete autonomy for people to make their own choices. People aren't allowed to do things that are harmful to other people, like driving drunk or throwing your trash into your neighbor's yard. Society generally recognizes the right of people in certain religions to oppose medical treatments if those beliefs don't impinge upon others. But society may restrict individuals who aren't vaccinated from certain activities, such as attending public schools.[14]

---

14. After the 2019 measles outbreaks, public schools in New York City cracked down on student vaccinations. It was reported that the unvaccinated were primarily in some religious communities, even though the vaccine refusal was not based on the religion itself.
https://www.washingtonpost.com/national/health-science/new-york-city-vaccination-order-shines-spotlight-on-insular-jewish-community/2019/04/11/fd59b098-5bc3-11e9-a00e-050dc7b82693_story.html

> **Grandma Rule!**
>
> One instance where personal choice may be overruled is what I call the "Grandma Rule." In some close-knit, multigenerational families, the Grandma figure can essentially tell family members what to do. She might tell an adult grandchild that they *will* get vaccinated because it's what their clergy person recommended, or because it will protect their health, or just because!

The employees of the company I mentioned earlier in the chapter were fully able to choose between getting vaccinated or finding a new job. In the U.S., getting vaccinated – like many things in life – is generally a personal choice.[15] In other countries, getting COVID vaccinations was required for many people. But in the U.S., there are very few things that people must do. Not doing something may have consequences – like not being able to have certain jobs, or do certain things – but those are personal choices.

● ● ●

If you're talking with a friend who is spreading misinformation for altruistic reasons – because they are trying to help other people stay healthy and safe – discussing their **altruistic motivations** and the importance of personal choice could be productive. You can ask them where they think people should get helpful information, while noting that everyone is different and should be able to make their own choices and decisions. Make it clear that you support their autonomy and right to share their (mis)information. Once they realize that sharing misinformation is in conflict with their desire to help people be healthy and stay safe, they

---

15. Members of the military are required to get certain vaccinations.

may start to question the misinformation, and stop sharing it.[16] That change is possible because altruistic spreaders aren't spreading misinformation for financial or other reasons, so they have a looser grip on their misinformation.[17]

The Ask-Tell-Ask Framework Can Lead to Deeper Discussions

The next step in your motivationally-focused conversations with misinformed friends is to use an Ask-Tell-Ask framework.[18] You – as a trusted messenger – ASK your friend for permission to discuss an issue, and then TELL them some insights from a third-party source. Then you ASK how they feel about that new perspective.

This three-step process is like being invited into someone's house. As a guest in their home, it would be inappropriate to give unsolicited advice about their lifestyle or decorating choices. That would build barriers, rather than enhancing trust and empathy.

The ASK part could start with a question like "Can we talk about _____ so I can understand it better?"

The "Tell" part of the process involves telling them something in the form of a question. (And no this is not like the TV show Jeopardy!®) This "telling" is giving them a piece of information from a

---

16. I know someone who would share all sorts of "health" information on social media, like what types of oils are healthy. Because of their actions, some of the people they trust suggested that their sources were not great, and they should look at snopes.com or check websites like Mayo clinic or WebMD, to verify that what they were sharing was accurate. This resulted in them not sharing as much questionable information.

17. You may recall this from Chapter 1.

18. This is a somewhat simplified version of the Ask-Tell-Ask process used by clinicians, and is also referred to as the "Elicit-Provide-Elicit" process. See "Using motivational interviewing and brief action planning for adopting and maintaining positive health behaviors," Progress in Cardiovascular Disease, 2023 https://www.sciencedirect.com/science/article/pii/S0033062023000099, and the Centre for Collaboration, Motivation and Innovation's "Ask-Tell-Ask: An Effective Way to Give Information and Advice, 2018 https://centrecmi.ca/wp-content/uploads/2019/03/12-Ask_Tell_Ask_2018-12-21.pdf

third party that they should find acceptable. This could be phrased as, "Would you be surprised if I told you that [trusted third-party source] said _____ about vaccines/COVID?" A trusted third-party could be a member of the clergy, a local business leader, a mutual friend, or a barber/hair stylist. This process is more like dancing (which is collaborative) than boxing, which is combative.

The final ASK is when you elicit a deeper response about the piece of information you put forward in the TELL part. This can be as simple as the open-ended question, "What do you think about that? How does it make you feel?" You can also couch this ASK in a bit of humor, with a question like, "It is a chaotic world with so many people believing such different things – what do you think about that?"

You can – and probably should – use the Ask-Tell-Ask technique repeatedly, as you continue your conversations.

Ask-Tell-Ask Example from Election Misinformation

An example of the Tell part of Ask-Tell-Ask process came to me from a work colleague "Bob" whose childhood friend insisted an election had been stolen because the lead had flipped overnight. "Bob" knew the former head of the state party that had lost the election and asked him whether he thought there was any fraud. The former party official said no, his party had lost the election because the other side did a better job of getting people out to vote. When "Bob" told that to their misinformed friend, it may not have convinced them that the election was squeaky clean, but they stopped insisting that the election had been stolen. This improved their relationship, and may have reduced the spread of election misinformation.

Trusted Allies Accelerate the Reversal of Misinformation

As we know, moving misinformed people off their misinformation is not quick or straightforward. You need to have many discussions with the misinformed person. **To make your discussions more effective, you can enlist trusted allies who can bring in complementary insights.** The more your friend trusts the messenger, the fewer times they need to hear the messages in order to loosen their grip on misinformation. Remember the Grandma rule – as a highly trusted and influential source, someone's grandmother may only need to say something once before it's acted upon.

Before you bring in a trusted ally, ask your friend's permission. Then you can bring your other friend, family member, or co-worker into the discussion. The trusted ally needs to understand how to have motivationally-focused conversations, and must agree NOT to present facts to correct your misinformed friend, or treat it as some sort of intervention.

1+1 = 3

In a research project I helped direct in January 2021, a group of college students assessed ways to reduce the sharing of misinformation on social media. One of the group's tactics was to have several students enter the same social media discussion to reinforce each other's statements that questioned the misinformation. Using this "swarm tactic" seemed to make other people in the discussion more likely to acknowledge the validity of the student's statements and less likely to blindly accept the misinformation.

You Want To Have One-on-One Conversations – NOT Public Group Discussions

A public gathering is not the right setting for a motivationally-focused conversation with a misinformed friend. The danger is that some members of the group might jump in with "correcting" facts rather than supporting a discussion that starts with listening and non-judgmental questions.

So, if someone brings up a piece of contentious misinformation at a family dinner, cocktail party, or work setting, it will be very difficult for you (if not impossible) to prevent others from challenging the misinformation. This will – of course – lead to a counter-productive "my facts v. your facts" argument.

Your goal in that type of situation is to terminate the non-productive, friction-escalating group discussion. You want to defuse the tension and try to meet later with the misinformed person.

To move the group away from the misinformation topic, you can try redirecting the discussion with something like, **"How 'bout them Mets?"** (or whatever sports team appeals to the group). Or you can try saying something like "This is a very controversial subject, and this is not the time or place to be talking about it." If there are children in the room, you could say, "This is not an appropriate discussion with children present."

Your goal is to lower the temperature and take the high road.

There is a chance that some people in the group won't let the topic go. If you're unable to redirect the discussion, your choices are limited. One option is to say, "I don't want to be part of this argument, so I'm going to leave." That may prompt someone with more authority in the group (perhaps the host, head of the household, or senior work person) to intervene and ask that the topic be off-limits so you won't leave.

If the person who brought up the misinformation in the group is a friend and you can find a way to talk with them alone, you could say, "This isn't the best place/time for this topic. Could we find a time later this week to continue our conversation with just the two of us?"

•••

Long-COVID is a Wild Card

Although millions of people in the U.S. are suffering prolonged problems after having had COVID, people who spread misinformation may claim that Long-COVID does not exist.

Discussions of Long-COVID with people who tend to believe misinformation can be complicated, because Long-COVID seems to involve at least three different pathological processes: immune system dysregulation, slow healing of damage caused by the viral infection (like scarring in the lungs), and perhaps some persistent viral infection. Those situations may co-exist in some people.[19]

Despite the complicated picture of Long-COVID, it can be a useful topic of conversation with people who have been misinformed – especially if they think that COVID is no worse than the flu. They may assume that Long-COVID only happens to people who are older or have other serious health issues, or that people with Long-COVID are lazy or pretending to be ill. In reality, COVID can leave healthy people debilitated and unable to do many things they could do before getting infected with the SARS-CoV2 virus.

For misinformed people who are concerned about the **economy**, noting that there are millions of people in the U.S. who are out of work because of Long-COVID could lead to productive conversations. You could say, "I've been wondering about the Long-COVID problem. I've heard that it is leaving many people unable to work and is hurting the economy. What do you think about that?"

•••

---

[19]. Fortunately, scientists are working to understand what is causing Long-COVID and how to treat it. An additional benefit of their work is that it should help people suffering with other forms of post-infection long-term health problems, like the so-called Chronic Lyme.

Examples of productive conversations with misinformed and vaccine-reluctant people

Below are two vignettes of productive discussions people have had with their family and co-workers using the concepts described above. The names of people and organizations in the vignettes below and in other sections of this book have been changed to protect their privacy.

> **Tell Me Your Success Stories**
>
> If you've had conversations with misinformed people that have led them to loosen their grip on misinformation – or abandon it completely – and you'd like me to consider including your story in a future edition of this book (or sharing it in other ways), please contact me at RevMisinfo@HealthPolCom.com.

• • •

1. Community Service Organization's Communications to Support Vaccine Confidence

A.B. is the leader of an urban non-profit organization that provides food services through two main facilities and some satellite locations, such as schools. Most of the employees are people of color, but A.B. is not.[20] At the start of the COVID-19 pandemic, the organization's goals were to keep people healthy and at work, and to maintain the organization's culture of caring for each other and the community.

A.B. managed the challenges of the COVID pandemic from a strong position of trust because of his over 15 years working at the organization. As a leader, he had been very hands-on, doing all manner of jobs including cooking, packaging, and loading and unloading trucks.

---

20. Because vaccines, COVID and related issues have become so controversial and fractious, names and locations are not specified.

He had also participated in a multi-day protest concerning how the organization's work wasn't being properly recognized and compensated by the local government, which was a major client.

To accomplish the organization's immediate goals of keeping everyone safe and employed, A.B. put COVID safety measures and activities in place. They organized people into work pods that could be socially distanced from each other, required masking, and quickly got extra gloves and masks from their normal suppliers.

In the early summer of 2020, as vaccines for COVID-19 were under development, an employee – who came to the organization through their food preparation training program and had been an employee for four years – asked A.B. "Are you going to accept the vaccinations? And are we going to have get vaccinated?" When he responded "Yes," she replied "No, No, No! Those vaccines will kill you."

A.B. considers this his "Ah-ha!" moment. It was when he realized that many of the organization's employees likely had similar levels of resistance to getting vaccinated stemming from structural inequities in health care delivery that they (or their families) may have encountered in their lives of for historical reasons.[21]

The level of mistrust of health care among his employees became even clearer for A.B. when an employee (who was comfortable with getting

---

21. Structural and systemic racism in the U.S. health care system have been analyzed by various groups, and the COVID-19 pandemic "amplified the harsh reality of health inequities experienced by racial and ethnic minority groups in the United States." https://www.healthaffairs.org/doi/10.1377/hlthaff.2021.01466 and https://www.ama-assn.org/delivering-care/health-equity/what-structural-racism Health care inequities and bias have been observed at the individual provider level, in financing and reimbursement methods, and in how health care is organized and delivered. There can also be bias in how treatments and diagnostic tests are developed, which can potentially make them less reliable for individuals of certain ethnic and racial groups. https://www.urban.org/research/publication/conceptual-map-structural-racism-health-care, https://www.stkate.edu/academics/healthcare-degrees/racism-in-healthcare, and https://www.tuskegee.edu/about-us/centers-of-excellence/bioethics-center/about-the-usphs-syphilis-study

vaccinated) told him that, "You're going to get a different vaccine than they're going to give me." Although A.B. assured them that this wasn't the case, it was unclear whether his statement was enough to change their perspective on racial inequities in the delivery of health care.

Such deeply-held mistrust was also recognized by the organization's head of human resources, X.Y., who is a woman of color. Because of that, she said, the organization's approach to COVID-19 had the "intentionality of recognizing the history of vaccine issues in health care for the black community."

To address their employees' concerns about COVID-19, and to maintain and build mutual trust, A.B. and other members of the leadership team created policies and regular opportunities for ongoing dialogue and active listening across the organization:

- Bringing in lunch every other week at both facilities so people could talk among themselves and with A.B. about their concerns related to COVID and other important issues of the day, including the killing of George Floyd.[22]

- A.B. regularly met one-on-one with a core group of long-standing employees who were widely trusted by other employees. (This group included both production employees and managers.) Those conversations helped A.B. stay closely aware of employees' concerns.

- If an employee had symptoms and tested positive for COVID (once testing became readily available), everyone in their work pod was required to isolate and received paid time off.[23]

---

22. George Floyd was a black man killed by police in Minneapolis on May 25, 2020 after being accused of using a counterfeit $20 bill. The four police officers were fired and later convicted and sent to jail for terms ranging from 3 to 22.5 years. https://www.nytimes.com/article/george-floyd.html and https://en.wikipedia.org/wiki/Murder_of_George_Floyd

23. Routine surveillance testing once or twice a week – like some health care and educational institutions did during the pandemic – was not available to the organization.

A.B.'s consistent messaging through those engagements and policies was that the organization would "follow the science," and that once vaccines were widely available, everyone would need to get vaccinated to continue working there.

"At the beginning [of the pandemic] I said that vaccines would be mandatory to work here. I didn't know when, but it will come at some time. Every time there was a question about how sure I was about this, there was no equivocation. I didn't want anyone to be surprised that people weren't being given a choice and I didn't want to give the impression that we were taking a 'wait and see' approach."

The concerns that A.B. and X.Y. had about employees' vaccine hesitancy and misinformation were borne out in a survey the organization did in January 2021, just after COVID vaccines were authorized by the FDA, but before they became widely available. A key finding was that 52% answered "No" to this question: "When the vaccine to prevent COVID-19 becomes available to you, will you get it?"

Other critical insights from the survey included:

- 52% did not believe the COVID-19 vaccines were safe. One respondent added that "The vaccine is not good, [and] I heard it made people sick [and] people dying of that COVID-19 vaccine..."

- 45% said that in general, vaccines made them nervous

- 42% agreed with the statement "Because of a history of racism, unethical experimentation, and questionable practices in drug development in communities of color, I do not trust the COVID-19 vaccine."

As the pandemic progressed and vaccines became available, A.B. and his team conducted the following activities to address employees' concerns about COVID vaccines:

- They held four Town Hall meetings with clinician leaders of color from a local health system. These were conducted on-line and at various times so all employees would be able to attend at least one of them. Computers were set up in conference rooms so people who might not have the ability to view them from home could join the on-line events from the organization's facilities. X.Y. noted that they created Town Hall meetings and other forms of engagement because it was clear that people were coming with "curious minds." In fact, one of the employees attended all four Town Hall meetings because they wanted to "hear everything."

- When it became clear that vaccines were going to be available, employees were prioritized by age for getting vaccinated at a clinic near the organization's main facility. When the clinic had extra doses at the end of each day, the employees working that day were offered the vaccines. To foster support for vaccinations, photos of employees getting vaccinated were shared within the organization, which created positive attitudes and excitement among the employees.

- Employees were given a paid day off to get vaccinated, which they could also use for the day after they got vaccinated if they were concerned about having a reaction.

- Early in the summer of 2021, as the date the organization had set for requiring vaccinations was approaching, they held a raffle among vaccinated employees, offering several $500 prizes to incentivize those who hadn't been vaccinated. They held weekly raffles from then on with $100 prizes until the cut-off date.[24]

X.Y. noted that, "A lot of our approach was about empowerment – empowering employees to make a decision. If your decision is to not get vaccinated, that's your choice – but our priority is to ensure the health of our employees and community."

<u>Rough Patches and Responses</u>

- Close to the vaccination requirement date, an employee who had been vocal about their no-vaccination position presented a card showing they'd been vaccinated several weeks ago. When asked about the card, they quickly admitted that it was fake.[25] From then on, proof of vaccination from a pharmacy or clinician's office was required in addition to the vaccine card.

- Another employee who presented a fake vaccination card admitted that they had done so because they were nervous about getting vaccinated. They agreed to get vaccinated, and there were no repercussions, because as X.Y. noted, "A big part of our success was the grace with which the organization approached the situation: recognizing that people were coming from different places and meeting them where they were."

---

24. Cash payment to everyone who got vaccinated was seen as coercive early in the pandemic, so the raffles were held instead. The organization's commitment to providing incentives continued, with additional $100 raffles for those who had the COVID-19 boosters, and direct $10 payments for getting the COVID-19 boosters, as well as for the flu and RSV vaccinations. (Also see "Challenges of Offering Financial Incentives for Vaccinations" in this Chapter's Appendix)

25. This employee did not get vaccinated and left their job.

Insights & Outcomes

A.B. concluded that "The attitude and culture we achieved may not have been that everyone was *excited* to get vaccinated, but people got comfortable with it."

"Even though I was the boss, because of the long-standing relationship I had with everyone, I was a trusted messenger. As a trusted person, the information and perspectives I brought to our formal and informal conversations – and the people we brought in to speak with the employees – resonated with our employees and staff. So when vaccinations became a requirement for employment, less than a handful of our almost 200 people elected to leave."

The organization had no deaths and no hospitalizations. A.B. concluded that *"I know that what we did saved lives, not just among our employees, but in their families, who I also believe were motivated to get vaccinated because of what we did in the workplace to dispel misinformation and promote vaccinations. Overall, I'm very proud of how we as a collective group of people responded to the crisis. We kept people at work. And we kept our people safe and made them more aware of things they could do to be healthier in the long run."*

Key Takeaways

- Although A.B. was the boss, he was also a trusted messenger.

- A.B. engaged in extensive active listening and proactive communications.

- The organization's leadership and internal culture leaders were aligned and consistent in their messaging.

- A.B. and the organization's leadership "met the employees where they were," approaching them with empathy and respect – and they were firm in establishing protocols based on science.

- The organization made it clear that the policies were put in place to promote and protect everyone's health and safety, not because of A.B.'s personal interest or the financial success of the organization.

• • •

2. Overcoming Vaccine Resistance: "My Sister and Her Kids"

C.D.'s sister E.F. had reasons to be anxious about health care and vaccines. Before COVID, E.F. had underlying anxiety about health care and dying. Not only did she have a fear of needles, but her father had died when she was a teenager, and her husband died in his early 40s, leaving her a single parent. She had also had two close encounters with mass traumatic events.

The COVID-19 pandemic only heightened her concerns of dying and fear of leaving her 9-year-old daughter and teenage son parentless. Her kids shared some of her concern, having lost their father when they were young.

As COVID vaccines became available, E.F.'s anxiety about vaccines was boosted by misinformation. She heard that the vaccines could cause heart problems in adolescent boys,[26] and could cause young girls to start getting their period early.

The suburban community in which she lived was also a bit of a bubble, with some "group-think" among moms who reinforced each other's concerns about the COVID vaccine causing early onset of puberty in their daughters. E.F. and her peers did not allow their daughters to get vaccinated.

C.D. wanted to address her sister's concerns about getting vaccinat-

---

26. While there was some evidence of myocarditis in younger males from the mRNA vaccines, the risks of that specific heart issue occurring were greater from COVID-19 than from the vaccine.

ed. She was persistent in having ongoing conversations with E.F., and brought in their older sister to reinforce the messaging. C.D. said that her sister "fundamentally believed that she should get vaccinated," but all the emotional and social barriers were blocking her from getting comfortable with the idea.

C.D. initially tried talking to E.F. about how "COVID is a dangerous thing," and told her she needed to get vaccinated to help stop the spread of the pandemic: "Do it for the common good." C.D. also suggested that her sister talk to her doctor and her children's pediatrician, but E.F. was not motivated to do that.

It soon became clear to C.D. that talking to her sister about facts was not effective. She then appealed to E.F.'s emotions and motivations – and particularly her concern for her kids – by saying, "You should do it for the kids" and "Your kids are nervous and worried about you." Around the same time, E.F was dipping into the world of on-line dating, and had connected with someone who would only date people who'd been vaccinated. E.F. and her kids also had to miss holiday gatherings with the family, and not surprisingly, "the kids were not happy about that."

E.F.'s major motivations included taking care of her kids – both physically and emotionally – and her own desire to have a broader social life. Those two internal motivators were powerful forces that could be reinforced by trusted messengers.

One major remaining obstacle was her fear of needles. Fortunately, one of E.F.'s friends was a local pharmacist. E.F. might not have trusted another clinician, but she was willing to listen to her pharmacist friend because there was an existing level of trust. The pharmacist friend reinforced C.D.'s messaging and agreed to personally give E.F. the vaccinations – and to do so in the thigh rather than the arm, which was more acceptable to E.F.[27]

Outcomes

- "Things aggregated," the persistence and consistent messaging from C.D. and their older sister finally resulted in E.F. receiving a COVID vaccination.

- Although E.F. got vaccinated, as did her son (eventually), her son only got a booster so he could go on college tours in the middle of the COVID pandemic. And because E.F. had residual concerns about vaccines and puberty and fertility, she didn't allow her daughter to get vaccinated. Her daughter eventually got COVID – fortunately with no long-term problems.

Key Take-Aways

- C.D.'s discussions with E.F. that focused on empathy and fundamental motivations were much more effective than trying to convince E.F. that she didn't understand the facts about vaccines and community health.

- C.D.'s persistence in having the discussions was key, as was enlisting other trusted messengers: their other sister and their pharmacist-friend. E.F.'s kids' concerns about their mom's health and fear of losing her connected to E.F.'s emotional motivations and reduced her resistance to getting vaccinated.

- Despite these efforts, E.F. continued to believe the misinformation about the effect of vaccines on younger girls.

• • •

---

27. This may relate to body autonomy, as the thigh is farther from the head, eyes and heart than the upper arm. Agreeing to receive the injection in an alternate site may also have given E.F. a greater sense of control.

Summary & Conclusions

- As a **trusted messenger** you can help your misinformed friends question their misinformation, and travel a path to rejecting it.

- Having these conversations will **reduce the friction in your relationships** and lead misinformed people to loosen their grip on misinformation. This will make them less likely to spread the misinformation, and more likely to do things like getting vaccinated.

- Having productive discussions with a misinformed friend, family member or co-worker involves active listening and **asking non-judgmental questions**. If you focus on their motivations and use your shared history, you can move the conversation down a better path over time.

- The **Ask-Tell-Ask process** can help someone consider new possibilities and perspectives by introducing them to insights from people they trust.

- Changes are **not going to happen simply or rapidly**. You will need to engage with your friend, family member of co-worker multiple times, with each discussion building on your previous conversations.

- The process can be more effective – and faster – if you bring in mutual friends who are **trusted allies** to reinforce your non-judgmental questions and expand the motivationally based conversations.

- If someone raises misinformation in a group setting it will likely lead to a "my facts v. your facts argument." Try to **defuse the tension** by changing the topic. You can then try to arrange a one-on-one conversation with them at another time.

Notes for Talking With Misinformed Friends

My misinformed friends, family or co-workers _____

Major topic [Friend #1] is misinformed about _____

Major Reasons [Friend #1] is Misinformed:

• Mistrust about X, Y, Z _____

• Historical or family experience _____

• Feeling that their autonomy is threatened by _____

Non-judgmental questions to ask [Friend #1] ("Can you tell me more about that?")
_____

Ask > Tell > Ask Process:•
 Ask permission to talk about _____

• Tell information in a non-judgmental way as a question; "Would
it surprise you to hear that [Another Respected Person] said?"
_____

• Ask follow-up questions to guide your discussion back to the misinformation
_____

Enlist mutual friends/trusted allies to reinforce you questions and discussion
_____

• Thank you for sharing your insights with me.
• I'd really like to continue our discussion soon.
• I'd like to ask [Trusted Ally] to talk about this with us. Do you think that would be OK?

Appendix to Chapter 2

Have You Met People? People are Complicated!

One of my favorite sayings, when someone is dismayed at someone else's words or actions is, "Have you met people?"

There is a wide range of things that people will do or think. Just because someone acts differently – or makes different life choices – from you, it doesn't mean they are crazy, bad or wrong.

People have the autonomy to make different decisions – as long as they aren't breaking laws or major social norms. In many parts of Vermont, for example, public nudity is legal, and some people choose to be unclothed in situations that many people would find odd, such as going into a store for a cup of coffee.[1] Unless that person is acting in a lewd or threatening manner, they probably aren't breaking any local laws. They're acting within the social norms embodied in those laws (pun intended) – even though that behavior might be illegal in other places.

A similar example might involve two people who live in very different ways: one has a very cluttered house while the other's house is extremely well ordered. Each person might think the other is strange, and not understand how the other person lives like that. At the extreme, their behavior might signal a pathology such as **hoarding disorder**[2] or **obsessive-compulsive disorder**.[3] But for people without disorders, the way they live simply reflects their preferences, and perhaps how they process information. For instance, some creative people, may be

---

1. https://fox8.com/news/naked-man-walks-into-vermont-store-buys-coffee/ (Accessed 2/20/2023) https://www.mychamplainvalley.com/news/police-chief-others-react-to-naked-man-in-downtown-burlington/ (Accessed 2/20/2023)

2. https://www.mayoclinic.org/diseases-conditions/hoarding-disorder/symptoms-causes/syc-20356056 (Accessed 2/20/2023)

3. https://www.mayoclinic.org/diseases-conditions/obsessive-compulsive-disorder/symptoms-causes/syc-20354432 (Accessed 2/20/2023)

comfortable living in a less well-ordered environment.[4]

"Understanding some people is like smelling the color nine" is one of my favorite sayings about how it can be difficult for us to connect on an intellectual or emotional level with some people's actions or beliefs that are very different from our own. That can be a challenge in our relationships, but it doesn't have to be an end, it can be a beginning – What does the color nine smell like to some people?

Different doesn't mean wrong or bad.

• • •

Challenges of Offering Financial Incentives for Vaccinations

Offering cash or a gift card is one way of inducing people to get vaccinated. Some employers have offered employees paid time off while then get vaccinated or for afterward, if have a reaction to the vaccine.[5] Both types of financial incentives have been criticized as being coercive.

A person susceptible to believing misinformation could feel that the incentive was challenging their autonomy. It might also increase their mistrust of the vaccine or of those offering the incentive.

How a misinformed person perceives the incentive will depend on where it is coming from. If it's being offered by the state government, an employer, or a large company, that could raise questions like, "Why are they paying me to get this shot I don't want? This is just another way for them to control me." And "What's in it for them?" But if a trusted community organization offered the incentive – like free bowling at the

---

4. https://www.lifehack.org/454661/messy-people-have-more-creative-and-productive-minds-science-says, and https://www.apa.org/monitor/2013/10/messy-desk (Accessed 2/20/2023)

5. Fever, headaches, muscle aches may occur after a vaccination. They are signs that the immune system is responding to the vaccine. This insight may be important when talking to people who are hesitant about the vaccine.

local lanes or free admission at the zoo[6] – that might be viewed more positively.

---

6. https://newbedfordlight.org/new-bedford-announces-walk-up-vaccine-clinics/

CHAPTER 3

TALKING WITH MISINFORMED STRANGERS

Interacting with misinformed people you don't know is a very different challenge from having motivationally-based conversations with people in your sphere of trust.

You may encounter misinformed people at gatherings of friends, a community event, or public places like parks or beaches. They may make a misinformed statement about vaccines or COVID, or they may confront you because you are wearing a mask or a vaccine-related t-shirt, hat or button. Or they may overhear you talking about COVID or vaccines – or something similar – and confront you because they want to "correct" you.

Common COVID-Related Misinformed Statements

Some of the misinformation you may hear:
- "Vaccines have killed more people than COVID."

- "The vaccines don't work. They're just a way for the government to control us and make the drug industry rich."

- "COVID is no worse than the flu. The government was saying COVID was very serious so they enforce a lock-down and control people, and put everyone out of work, so ordinary people would be reliant on government hand-outs and bail-outs."

- "Masks don't work. They just make people sick by trapping CO_2 and breeding germs."

Your first priority is your safety – whether you are in a group setting or confronted by someone one-on-one.

How you respond to misinformed statements depend on the situation. If you are in a one-on-one conversation, or encounter a misinformed person at a group event such as a neighborhood block party, there will be different challenges and opportunities. In a group setting (as noted in Chapter 2), it is unlikely that you'll be able to engage them in a productive conversation because other people in the group may try to correct their misinformation. As we know, correcting their misinformation will harden their belief in the misinformation, and likely lead to a "my facts v. your facts" argument – and could even result in verbally abusive or physically threatening situations.

Personal safety in the post-COVID world needs to be taken very seriously. The COVID-19 pandemic seems to have made some people lose their sense of normal social behaviors. Uncivil statements and attitudes have spilled over from social media into real life, with some people acting aggressively, and without regard to other people's feelings or personal space.[1] When you are confronted by someone spouting misinformation, your first priority is your own safety, so the best thing you can do is to not engage with them.

In those types of situations, your choices depend upon whether you can easily remove yourself from their presence (like in a park), or if you cannot leave (like in an airplane). If you can separate yourself from this person, say something like "Thank you" and "I see" before putting some physical distance between you and that person. If you cannot easily separate yourself from them, then a short series of non-judgmental questions or leading statements like "Tell me more about that," or "Interesting. Where did you hear that?" may be a wise choice. You can end the interaction by saying something like "Thanks. You've given me some things to think about." And "I'm sorry, but I need to read something for work" (or respond to an email, or take a nap).

• • •

If someone won't leave you alone about their misinformation, and they are badgering or harassing you, or you feel threatened – remember that you don't know them, their history, motivations, or why they mistrust experts. In those situations you have several options. If they seem particularly adamant about sharing their misinformation, **you can try responding with "That sounds right" to defuse the situation and disengage.** But to maintain your own sense of internal balance, you can also say to yourself (in your head, not out loud!), "That sounds right to *you*!"

---

1. "Are people more disrespectful, unkind since the pandemic? Experts say yes and here's why," CBS News, 10/23/23 - https://www.cbsnews.com/miami/news/are-people-more-disrespectful-unkind-since-the-pandemic-experts-say-yes-and-heres-why/; "Public freakouts, burnout, and bullying: Bad behavior is here to stay," Axios, 9/1/23 - https://www.axios.com/2023/09/01/covid-pandemic-mental-heallth-crisis-public-freakouts; "Americans have forgotten how to behave. And it's time to stop blaming the pandemic," LA Times, 8/17/23 - https://www.latimes.com/entertainment-arts/story/2023-08-17/concerts-movies-airplanes-restaurants-theme-parks-bad-behavior-theory-column; and "Why Can't People Be Normal in Public Anymore?," Vice, 2/5/24 - https://www.vice.com/en/article/qjvaex/why-are-people-acting-out-in-public

Another alternative – if they don't seem especially adamant or threatening – is to engage with them by asking non-judgmental questions. You could use the Ask-Tell-Ask process to better understand their misinformed reality. The insights or anecdotes from those conversations might help you broaden the scope of your discussions with misinformed friends. For example, you could tell a friend who believes vaccines cause autism or infertility about a conversation you had with a stranger who thinks Ivermectin can cure COVID. Then ask your friend what they think about that, which could give you a point of agreement – if they recognize that Ivermectin is not a cure for COVID-19.

Misinformed People Are Everywhere

Late in 2023, I had a virtual meeting with someone I'd met at an online networking event, to get advice about on-line marketing. Our meeting started with them telling me how important it was to use AI, but they quickly moved on to how the COVID-19 vaccines were just a scam to make money for big pharmaceutical companies blah blah blah. I then asked them some non-judgmental questions about their statements and where they'd heard those things. They said that I should search the internet. In response to my asking what websites I should look at, since searching for that sort of "information" returned millions of results, they said, "just keep scrolling down."

This is a classic example of confirmation bias. They only accept information that is consistent with what they already believe, and they reject any contrary information and sources.

• • •

It is possible to reverse misinformation with people you don't know, using the techniques described in Chapter 2. However, you would have to develop some type of positive relationship and trust. An example of this happening is from the 1980s: Daryl Davis, a black musician from Maryland, successfully engaged with members and leaders of the Ku Klux Klan, resulting in them renouncing their beliefs in white supremacy. As Daryl stated in a 2007 NPR interview, "As you build upon those commonalities, you're forming a relationship, and as you build about that relationship, you're forming a friendship. That's what would happen. I didn't convert anybody. They saw the light and converted themselves."[2]

This is a great illustration of how someone – if they choose to – can engage with strangers and change their minds. Mr. Davis embraced people with empathy, met them where they were, and used the principles of motivational interviewing to achieve dramatic results. His experience of becoming a trusted messenger with strangers who held seriously "problematic" beliefs is very inspiring.

However, it is important to recognize that Mr. Davis' experience occurred well before social media existed. The landscape of social discourse is now very different than it was in the 1980s. Not only have social media, podcasts and niche information sources proliferated, but physical attacks against strangers seem to be rising. Pursuing this type of action with misinformed strangers should be approached very cautiously.

Summary & Conclusions

- Interacting with misinformed strangers is very different from having productive conversations with people you know. You don't know their history or motivations, and because they don't know you, there is no inherent level of trust and shared history to build upon.

---

2. https://www.npr.org/2017/08/20/544861933/how-one-man-convinced-200-ku-klux-klan-members-to-give-up-their-robes,
Also see Ted Talk: https://www.ted.com/talks/daryl_davis_why_i_as_a_black_man_attend_kkk_rallies?language=en

- **Your safety is your first priority when engaging with misinformed strangers.**

- How you respond to misinformed strangers depends on whether you are in a group setting or are in a one-on-one conversation. Your decision should also depend on whether you're in a location you can leave – like a public park – or someplace you cannot leave, like an airplane, or you don't want to leave, like a family gathering (or an expensive seat at a sports arena).

- Since your safety is paramount, your best option may be to deflect the discussion to another topic, or ask a few non-judgmental questions and end the conversation - "I really want to watch the game."

Chapter 4

Preventing & Reversing Misinformation in Communities

It takes a village.

This chapter explores how you can help prevent and reverse misinformation in your community. It is important because misinformation can create societal friction and decrease economic growth.

The first three sections of this chapter describe:

1. How promoting **community activity to prevent and reverse misinformation** is different from having one-on-one discussions with a misinformed friend.

2. Ways you can **prevent** misinformation from taking hold in people (particularly in children) if they are exposed to it.

3. How to **contain and reverse misinformation** after it starts spreading.

The final sections explore higher-level actions you can take in your community. The chapter concludes with a notes page to help you organize your ideas and strategy.

Community Activity is a Team Sport

Chapters 1, 2 and 3 focused on how you can use one-on-one interactions to reduce the spread of misinformation and improve your relationships with misinformed people. Preventing and reversing misinformation in your community requires a different approach: engaging with **trusted allies** and other people you can partner with to raise awareness and advocate for changes.

Your allies don't need to be people with senior titles, they just need to be credible and trusted within the community. They can be clergy, business executives and owners, bartenders or baristas, government officials, educators, sports personalities, or anyone who is respected and listened to by many people.

And remember the Grandma Rule! In a community setting the "Grandma" role might be played by a revered coach or member of the clergy who can say, "I knew you when you were a kid" or, "I knew your parents/grandparents." Their shared history and position as a community leader could make them a **credible ally and a trusted messenger**.

How you choose what misinformation you want to reverse in your community will depend on what is spreading and causing harms. You should also consider who you might recruit as good allies and messengers. The important thing is to pick a specific piece of misinformation you believe you can defuse. Over-analysis can lead to delay and more harm, so you may want to embrace Nike's famous phrase, "Just Do It."[1]

---

1. "Just Do It." is a trademark of the Nike corporation. https://www.trademarkia.com/blogs/trending/nike-trademark-just-do-it

Preventing Misinformation in Your Community
==

Empowering people – particularly children – by teaching them how to identify and rebuff misinformation may be the best way to prevent them from being misinformed.

The key abilities that people need to identify and reject misinformation are:

1. **Understanding science and the scientific method:** A person who understands the scientific concept of cause and effect will recognize that **correlation does not prove causation.**[2]

2. **Critical thinking:** A person who thinks critically will be able to analyze problems and evaluate possible solutions. They can then develop and test hypotheses to evaluate different options.

3. **Media literacy** enables a person to evaluate information sources and distinguish those that are valid from those that are not.

Preventing people from embracing misinformation is much more effective than keeping it from spreading once it has taken root. Enabling people to recognize and deflect misinformation is sometimes called "prebunking."[3] One prebunking technique is to show people examples of misinformation so they are better able to recognize it in the future. Preventing misinformation about vaccines is sometimes called "vaccinating against misinformation."[4]

---

[2]. Perceived correlation is often how a truth nugget will morph into misinformation. People who understand the scientific process also appreciate that an experiment with negative results isn't a failure – it means you've learned something.

[3]. Prebunking is related to debunking. Prebunking is taking steps to prevent false statements from taking hold and spreading. Debunking is refuting false statements after they have spread.

[4]. "Vaccinating against misinformation" was the title of a panel I was on at the 2021 World Vaccine Congress. I moderated a similar session at the 2022 meeting in Washington, DC.

• • •

Since almost every community has schools,[5] encouraging more teaching of the key skills listed above is something you should strongly consider. Doing that will empower children to think for themselves, and could help them educate their parents and other adults.

People of all ages may have insufficient media literacy because information sources have multiplied and become more specialized.[6] The proliferation of information sources started several decades ago with talk radio and cable TV, then moved to the internet with blogs, podcasts, and social media platforms and channels such as YouTube, Facebook, X (Twitter), Reddit, TikTok, Telegram, Think Social! and Pinterest.[7] **We are literally living among silos of information.** Those siloed platforms allow almost anyone to have an "information channel" that looks like a reputable media source. To build their audience and boost revenue, many sources have narrowed their focus and viewpoint. (See Chapter 6 for more about social media and misinformation.)

• • •

How you raise awareness about the importance of preventing misinformation in your community will depend on your connections and the

---

5. Retirement communities may not have children or schools. They present a different set of challenges for preventing and reversing misinformation.

6. Younger people are reportedly getting much of their information from social media. "More Americans – especially young adults – are regularly getting news on TikTok," Pew Research Center, September 17, 2024 https://www.pewresearch.org/short-reads/2024/09/17/more-americans-regularly-get-news-on-tiktok-especially-young-adults/ (Accessed October 9, 2024). Only 20 years ago, they were reported to get most of their news from comedy shows, such as the Daily Show with Jon Stewart. "Young Get News from Comedy Central," CBS News, March 1, 2004 https://www.cbsnews.com/news/young-get-news-from-comedy-central/. As discussed in Chapter 6, content is regulated very differently for those two sources of information.

7. Note: "Pinterest's misinformation policy prohibits things like promotion of false cures for terminal or chronic illnesses and anti-vaccination advice." https://help.pinterest.com/en/article/health-misinformation (Accessed June 10, 2024)

current state of education in your area – particularly around media literacy. You will need to identify the people and organizations that can be your allies and help you influence education policies and practices. If you have school-age children, you may already have allies within the school system, such as a principal, superintendent, or members of the school board or PTA who may recognize that media literacy is a problem. Those potential partners are a great starting place for your conversations about the problems of misinformation and the benefits of "vaccinating" children against it.

To support your efforts to increase the teaching of media literacy (and science and critical thinking), you may also want to engage with community partners <u>outside</u> the school system. For example, business leaders who recognize the importance of having an educated local workforce should appreciate how misinformation can harm economic activity and the value of media literacy. To recruit those allies, talk with them about how misinformation can harm people and organizations in the community, how media literacy can prevent children from being infected with misinformation, and how misinformation harms economic growth and civility.

Media literacy can also be a problem for adults. Organizations in your community that could provide educational "prebunking" programs for adults include the public library, local community colleges, or workforce-development organizations. Those types of organizations are worth contacting to see how you can help, especially if you have connections to their senior staff.

Teaching media literacy for adults should be presented as a way to help them find accurate information about things they're interested in, such as their health, finances, weather, or elections. **Media literacy training for adults can be integrated into programs about how to avoid computer viruses, financial scams, and identity theft.**

• • •

You and your allies can raise awareness and advocate for **preventing children from being misinformed** by making statements at public meetings, writing letters to the editor, and calling in to local news shows.[8] Begin your statements and letters by recognizing common community goals such as, "We all want our kids to get good educations so they can get good jobs" – an approach that is non-confrontational. Next, highlight the harms misinformation can cause and discuss the benefits of teaching children about science, critical thinking, and media literacy.

The goal of promoting media literacy is to put more tools in the toolbox of teachers and librarians (and others) so they can help people differentiate valid and reliable sources of information from those that are not. The desired outcome from improved media literacy is that people will ask more and better questions about the validity of the information they are exposed to. Ideally, incentives will also be created for people to ask those questions. For teachers, that could mean evaluating students based on how well they scrutinize and validate their information sources.

This works at home as well. If parents ask their children about their information sources when the child makes statements that seem problematic. Those conversations should follow the same pathway as those described in Chapter 2. When parents hear something from their child that isn't correct, they can ask non-judgmental questions, which might lead their children to explain how they heard the misinformation. Productive conversation about the validity of media outlets and other information sources can help children evaluate what they hear and read in the future. That is the essence of "vaccinating against misinformation."

---

8. In some communities, public-access TV shows can be a way for you to raise awareness of issues and present ideas for positive change. Those outlets generally have low barriers to getting on the air and may be easy to work with.

As you advocate for expanding the teaching of media literacy skills, you may get pushback from educators who assert that it is already being taught as part of school's normal coursework. If that happens, you can use motivational conversation tactics and ask how they know the kids have a high level of media literacy. You can advocate for students' media literacy skills to be evaluated the same way reading and math skills are routinely tested. To make those evaluations more meaningful, they should be connected to incentives for teachers. Those are all things you can advocate for alone and with your community partners.

Teaching media literacy in schools probably should not be done in isolation. It will be more effective when integrated into the normal coursework of subjects like biology, social studies, and history.

• • •

Different generations trust very different information sources. An educator I spoke with noted that younger people turn to social media platforms such as TikTok where they develop long-term trust relationships. A child who trusts information from a TikTok influencer about a sports team or celebrity may trust the influencer's information about other topics, such as health, nutrition or elections.

An educator I spoke with noted that "teaching media literacy in schools is important because it is part of a comprehensive civics education, which is necessary for being a well-informed citizen." They also noted that teaching and firefighting both face challenges with technological advancements: Firefighters today need to know how to suppress lithium-ion batteries fires, and teachers need to know how to respond to students accessing – and believing – information from a broad array of sources, many of which may not be reliable or accurate.

Media Literacy Resources

There are many resources for teachers, school administrators, librarians, and parents.

- **Bureau of Education & Research** provides resources for educators, such as a course called "Teaching Media Literacy Skills in a Fake New World," https://www.ber.org/seminars/course/BL1/Teaching-MEDIA-LITERACY-SKILLS-in-a-Fake-News-World

- **Media Literacy Now** focuses on "policy change at local, state, and national levels in the U.S. to ensure all K-12 students are taught media literacy so that they become healthy, confident and competent media consumers and creators." https://medialiteracynow.org/about/mission/

- **News Literacy Project** is a non-profit foundation focusing on increasing news literacy so that people – particularly students – will have the "knowledge and ability to participate in civic society as well-informed, critical thinkers" https://newslit.org/

- **National Association of Independent Schools** has a variety of resources, including a May 2024 article about The Importance of Teaching Digital Citizenship that includes links to other resources https://www.nais.org/learn/independent-ideas/may-2024/the-importance-of-teaching-digital-citizenship/

- **The Trusted Web** is a coalition of 18 organizations working against fake news. https://thetrustedweb.org/organizations-leading-the-fight-against-fake-news/ Part of their work is the News Literacy Project. https://newslit.org/

• • •

At public meetings, your **credible local allies** can be particularly helpful. You can join forces with them in a variant of the "swarm tactic" that was discussed in Chapter 2. When you have the opportunity to make public comments – such as at town council or PTA meetings – your allies can reinforce your messages by adding their own non-judgmental questions and comments. Similarly, they can post supportive statements in on-line newspaper discussions, blogs, or local social-media platforms like Nextdoor.[9]

Reversing Misinformation in Your Community

Reversing misinformation is like beating down the flames after the fire has already started.

Your primary goal in reversing misinformation in your community is to stop people from accepting it, which will keep it from spreading.

Common topics of misinformation – vaccines, COVID and elections – seem to be present everywhere. Your community's misinformation may include specific issues based upon a local situation or geography. For example, people in southern states in the U.S. may be exposed to misinformation about border security or immigration, and people in rural areas may hear more misinformation about COVID treatments because they are familiar with veterinary medicine.[10]

The misinformation circulating in your area should be easy to identify since it will be in the news, a topic of local gossip, or on the agenda at

---

9. https://nextdoor.com/

10. Because rural areas have more direct exposure to agriculture, familiarity with the anti-parasitic deworming medication ivermectin that was – and still is – falsely claimed to be a cure or preventive measure for COVID. "Ivermectin: How false science created a Covid 'miracle' drug," BBC, 10/6/2021 https://www.bbc.com/news/health-58170809, and "Misinformation, Trust, and Use of Ivermectin and Hydroxychloroquine for COVID-19," JAMA, 9/29/2023 https://jamanetwork.com/journals/jama-health-forum/fullarticle/2809985

town council meetings. You can assess how it is harming your community: **is misinformation in your community undermining public health, education, civil discourse, or economic growth?**

• • •

How you reverse misinformation in your community will depend on what misinformation is circulating and who your best allies might be.

Your first step in finding allies is to identify people you know connected to organizations that can influence the spread of misinformation. You will need to talk with them first, to determine their interest in being **credible allies**. The closer they are to seeing the harms that misinformation causes, the more likely they may be interested in partnering with you. They can help **amplify your messages** about the dangers of the misinformation and join you in advocating for action.

Examples of misinformation about public health[11] that might be circulating and causing harm in your community include:

- **A new mask requirement** for people at health care facilities or schools

- A **proposed state or city law lowering the age of consent for receiving a vaccination**

- A proposal to **eliminate requirements for getting dogs vaccinated for rabies**[12] **and distemper**

---

11. I chose public health examples because those are what I know best, but misinformation could be about things like immigration or local zoning changes.

12. See https://www.npr.org/sections/health-shots/2023/10/11/1205016558/canine-vaccine-hesitancy-dogs-rabies and https://www.animallaw.info/topic/table-rabies-vaccination-laws

Trusted allies for reversing misinformation can work with you to identify opportunities for action, and help you make positive changes in your community. Your allies can be business owners; people on the Town Council or PTA; clergy leaders; individuals who work in local government, public health or media; or people running non-profit organizations like the United Way, VFW, 4H, and Rotary.

Your best allies will appreciate the harms misinformation is causing, and have connections to the organizations that can work with you to take positive actions. If the misinformation in your community is about a public health issue – like a requirement to wear masks – the public health agencies, hospitals and business owners could be important potential partners. And local business leaders and clinicians could be community allies. All of them would share your motivation to improve community health and economic viability, and may want to be part of your informal advocacy team.

Your potential teammates may not initially want to join you in trying to reverse misinformation. They may be happy to talk about and identify toxic misinformation in your community, but because the situation seems daunting, they may feel helpless or reluctant to take action. First, discuss the harm misinformation can cause, and ask them to help you identify opportunities for reversing misinformation. Then ask them about how serious the situation is, and whether reversing misinformation is important for them and the community: "Do you think that misinformation is harming our community?" Discussing aspects of that question can help motivate them to join you.

Example of New Mask Requirement

The truth nugget at the core of the misinformation about masks likely came from the start of the pandemic, when we didn't know the virus causing COVID was spread through the air. Because the science of the SARS-CoV-2 virus was still developing, the public was initially told they didn't need to wear masks. After scientists discovered that the virus was transmitted in the air, the public was told they shouldn't get masks because there was a shortage of the high-quality masks needed by health care workers and patients.

Those situations were spun into the misinformation that the "experts don't know anything" because they kept changing their recommendations (or were "hiding things"), and that masks didn't work or weren't needed. Later versions of mask misinformation were that masks spread germs, or caused a buildup of CO_2 that could be harmful.

If the rates of contagious respiratory illnesses rise in an area, the local hospital may be concerned that many of their employees could become ill, leaving them short-staffed. In those cases, hospitals[13] may put in place requirements for people in their buildings to wear masks.[14] Their motivation is to keep people healthy and for the hospital to be able to function at full capacity.

A community ally for supporting a new mask requirement could be the chief of police, because not only do masks can keep the police and other first responders safe, but a fully-functioning hospital is part of community safety. The police chief could publicly support a mask requirement by putting a notice on the department's website or social media pages, making a statement at a town council meeting or other public event, or writing a letter to the editor of the local paper.

The chief could also publicly state that the police department would help enforce the mask requirement at the hospital if a mask-refuser threatened or assaulted a hospital employee, patient or visitor. Of course, in some communities, the police chief may be seen as an

---

13. Schools could put in place mask requirements for similar reasons.

14. As happened at some hospitals at the end of the summer of 2024.

authority figure who is taking part in a "big government" move to "institute a police state around mask requirements." Or they may have close ties to community members who promote misinformation and mask refusal. You and your trusted allies should have insights about those possibilities.

Action Steps for Reversing Community Misinformation

As you **make statements and write letters** to reverse misinformation in your community, you will want to foster an empathic, positive conversation. Remember, your goal is to reduce the influence of misinformation in the community. Your actions should be similar to the type of one-on-one, motivationally-based conversations described in Chapter 2, but with a broader group of people.

For you to do this effectively, **you should use positive, inclusive phrases** such as, "We can all agree that we want our hospitals to be fully staffed to care for people with cancer or who have accidents." That way, you are starting with your community's shared motivation: you all want a safer, healthier, and more economically robust community. **You're focusing the discussion on the outcome, not challenging the misinformation.**

After establishing the community's shared goals, ask about – but don't challenge – their sources of misinformation. You could do that by posing a non-judgmental public question like, "I'd be interested in knowing where that information comes from?"

Some of the people who respond to that question may be the ones who are spreading misinformation. Since you don't want to engage in a "my facts v. your facts" debate, you should be ready for situations where spreaders of misinformation identify their sources with vague responses, like "The internet" or "Just google it and keep scrolling down" or "I heard it on a podcast." In those situations, you can respond by simply noting that those "sources" are very non-specific. If misinformation spreaders come back with more specific sources – particularly if it is a single source or several that are linked – you can respond using the concepts of media literacy. To do this, mention that their sources may not be valid because so few websites make the same claim, or the authors seem to have self-serving reasons for promoting their website or products.

You don't want to *challenge* their misinformation with facts – you want to illuminate the reality that their sources are suspect and invalid. It is possible that in a public discussion – whether live or through newspapers or local social media – some people in your community will chime in and try to refute the misinformation with facts. So you need to be prepared to tolerate some "facts v. facts" exchanges as you guide the community discussion in an empathetic and inclusive way.

• • •

If you are challenged to provide your sources or expertise – perhaps after you publicly question the "sources" provided by spreaders of misinformation – you can refer to experts in your community. Your local experts could be people in the health department, local hospital, or leading clinicians. Others who could provide support for the validity of these experts are community leaders, such as clergy and business owners.

In providing those sources – and using references to the scientific method (ideally without calling it that) – you can bridge the discussion to the basic motivations of healthy communities and vibrant economies: "The one thing all those people and organizations have in common is their desire for healthy communities with good jobs and a growing economy. Helping to prevent people from getting sick actually reduces income for some community members and organizations – like doctors and the hospital – who are clearly not acting out of self-interest."

While you may be accused of having been co-opted or "brainwashed" by "big medicine" or "big government," you will have established the landscape for dialogue. On one side are the legitimate local experts who should have broad community support – and on the other, murky social media or internet sources.

Sometimes, these tactics may not work – which is why you always need to understand a person's **motivations**. If the person is spreading misinformation because that is how they make **money** (such as a talk-radio host or a podcaster), or how they maintain their position of **power** (such as a politician), then directly engaging with them may not be useful or productive. In those situations, consider the old saying: "Don't wrestle with pigs. You both get dirty, and the pigs like it." You can try to deflate the discussion with statements like "Thinking people can disagree,"[15] and then disengage from the public dialogue so you don't give the misinformation a potentially larger platform.

Challenges of Reversing Misinformation

- Potential allies who could join you in seeking to reverse or deflate misinformation may be **afraid that they will be personally ridiculed or attacked**. Those are real concerns, but they need to be balanced against the real harm that misinformation creates for the community. If you work together, you can identify how to contain and reverse the misinformation.

- You and your allies want to illuminate and defuse the misinformation **without giving misinformation spreaders an enhanced platform.** Your goal is to foster a calm discussion, not an argument that spirals across the community.

- **Beware of being labeled.** You need to be prepared to respond if someone tries to label you as "One of those people who is (woke, communist, liberal, elitist, or pick another label)." You can

---

15. Hat-tip for this nugget to a senior history professor and academic leader.

respond as follows:

"Labels only stigmatize, dehumanize, or diminish people, and I'm not going to respond by labelling you. I'd rather we have a civil discussion about how to improve our community." Or **"Thinking people can disagree, but labels only reduce people to stereotypes, and none of us wants to be seen as a stereotype."**

Reversing Misinformation at the Next Level

A higher level of commitment to reversing misinformation is serving on a committee or board. That will give you a more influential position. You could serve on the board of a non-profit organization (including houses of worship) or a governmental organization like the PTA or Board of Health. You can also run for elected positions on the School Board or Town Council.

Other ways you can promote awareness about the toxicity of misinformation include organizing discussion groups about books such as those by Dr. Peter Hotez,[16] or hosting a screening of a documentary like "Shot in the Arm"[17] through your local cinema, library or public health group.

Directly Supporting Public Health Organizations

If you want to work on specific public health activities – such as **improving vaccination rates for children** – you can support your local and state public health agencies. How you do that will depend upon where you live and your local connections.

States, cities and towns have health departments, and state legislatures have health committees with jurisdiction over public health depart-

---

16. "Vaccines Did Not Cause Rachel's Autism," "Preventing the Next Pandemic," and "The Deadly Rise of Anti-Science" - https://peterhotez.org/book/, and https://www.amazon.com/Books-Peter-Hotez/s?rh=n%3A283155%2Cp_27%3APeter+Hotez

17. https://shotinthearmmovie.com/

ments and activities. You may know people who work in those organizations, or local media, or you may know community leaders who have an interest in public health. Local business leaders should also be supportive of public health because the COVID-19 pandemic showed them how important public health is for economic stability and growth.

Supporting public health groups is very important because many agencies were aggressively undermined during the COVID pandemic, and some had their authorities and budgets reduced dramatically.[18] That recent history may make them very receptive to your offer of help. You can find your city and county health departments through the National Association of County & City Health Officials' webpage directory: https://www.naccho.org/membership/lhd-directory.

There are also non-governmental groups that work to raise awareness and advocate for public health issues. The American Public Health Association has state affiliates: https://www.apha.org/apha-communities/affiliates/state-and-regional-public-health-associations. Other advocacy groups work on public health legislation. For example, the SAFE Communities Coalition is a group of states affiliates[19] that train people to advocate for legislation and regulations to increase childhood vaccination rates. If you are interested in engaging at that level, you can contact Safe Communities to find out how to get involved with their work.[20]

---

18. "Over Half of States Have Rolled Back Public Health Powers in Pandemic," KFF News, September 15, 2021 - https://kffhealthnews.org/news/article/over-half-of-states-have-rolled-back-public-health-powers-in-pandemic/. "Trends in US State Public Health Emergency Laws, 2021–2022," American Journal of Public Health, February 15, 2023 - https://ajph.aphapublications.org/doi/full/10.2105/AJPH.2022.307214

19. https://www.safecommunitiescoalition.org/chapters

20. https://secure.everyaction.com/ZmaW9hZNd0yFrRXZgxxLPw2

Summary & Conclusions

- You can be a **change agent and change leader** for preventing and reversing misinformation in your community.

- Unlike your one-on-one conversations with misinformed friends, family and co-workers, **community action is a team sport**. You need to partner with trusted allies. Who you partner with will depend on the misinformation topic and your team's community connections.

- **Your allies can be all manner of local leaders and change agents**: PTA members, business leaders, clergy, baristas, bartenders, and sports coaches. And don't forget the Grandmas because they do rule.

- **You can prevent misinformation from taking root by educating** children and adults about the scientific method, critical thinking, and media literacy – particularly how to discern valid sources from those that are spreading misinformation.

- Your first step in reversing existing misinformation is to **raise awareness about the harm** it is causing in your community.

- You can **raise awareness** in letters to the editor, and by making non-judgmental statements at public events like Town Council meetings. Raising awareness at those events will refute misinformation in your community, and prevent new misinformation from taking hold and spreading.

- Your **community allies can make supportive statements** at those meetings – or submit follow-up letters to the media – to amplify the impact of your messages.

- You and your community allies can undermine the spread of misinformation with **empathy** and by posting motivationally-focused questions.

- You and your allies **don't want to disparage misinformed people** and misinformation spreaders. You want to **collectively embrace them into change**.

- You can also **serve on local government committees** (such as the PTA), or even run for local office, like the City Council.

- You can **raise awareness of the dangers of misinformation** with your friends by organizing community discussions at a library, community center, coffee shop, or someone's home or office. Those discussions could be centered around relevant books, documentaries or articles.

- Your **local and state health departments should be delighted by your offer of support,** as would your state's public health association. They could point you toward other opportunities for supporting public health in your state and community.

Notes for Preventing & Reversing Community Misinformation

Ways I can promote education about science, critical thinking & media literacy
_____

Working with schools _____

Working with organizations that educate adults, such as libraries & community colleges
_____

Major topics of misinformation in my community _____

Community leaders I know who could be supportive allies, including business leaders, clergy, media, town council, PTA, and sports coaches _____

Non-judgmental questions to raise at public meetings or in letters to editor – particularly about sources behind misinformation _____

<u>Points to include in your public comments and letters</u>

- Thank you for what you're doing to make our community better

- Thank you for giving me the opportunity to share my questions about _____

- What should be our next steps concerning those issues?

- How do we identify credible information about those issues and reach some consensus?

Contact information for my local and state Public Health Agencies, and my state's Public Health Association _____

CHAPTER 5

ELECTION & CLIMATE CHANGE MISINFORMATION

Fake news makes news.[1]

You can have productive conversations with friends who've been misinformed about elections and climate change, as you would with friends who are misinformed about vaccines and COVID.

This chapter explores why some of your friends may be misinformed about elections and climate change, and how you can have productive, motivationally-focused conversations with them.[2]

The "how-to" strategies for talking with friends misinformed about elections or climate change are similar to those in Chapter 2.

---

1. Fake news was the Collins' dictionary Word of the Year in 2017 - https://www.bbc.com/news/uk-41838386

2. Talking about elections and politics with co-workers in the workplace or at work events may not be acceptable according to your organization's policies.

The first section of this chapter is about **election misinformation**:

- How election misinformation is different from political misinformation

- Who is spreading election misinformation, and likely sources of your friends' misinformation

- Why people are susceptible to election misinformation

- How to talk with friends who have been misinformed about elections

Later sections of the chapter cover misinformation about **climate change**.

You may encounter misinformation about elections and climate change during community activities, such as Town Council meetings about election technologies and practices, or storm and flood preparedness. For **community discussions**, use the principles and actions from Chapter 4.

Context will guide your strategy for how to reverse misinformation: are you discussing a piece of misinformation with someone you know, or with a broader group in your community? Or are you talking with someone you don't know?

If you're talking with someone you don't know who is misinformed about elections or climate change (or really anything else that they are passionate or agitated about), apply the principles and practices described in Chapter 3.

Remember, your **personal safety is your highest priority**, so in many cases your best option – if possible – is to disengage from any interactions with that person. If you cannot disengage, try to change the topic to something that isn't controversial, like a local sports team. That's the safest approach when you don't know their motivations or personal history, because **your personal safety is always your highest priority**.

Election Misinformation is Different From Political Misinformation

Misinformation about elections is different from – but related to – political misinformation.

Election misinformation is incorrect information about the election process. Political misinformation is much broader and can be about policy positions, specific legislation, political parties, nominees for appointed positions, another candidate, or the candidate's own experience.[3,4] The two meet when misinformation about the integrity of the election process is used for political purposes.

A key difference between election and political misinformation is the purpose of the misinformation. Election misinformation is focused on challenging the results of an election, while the objective of political misinformation can be to derail an opponent's campaign; to boost the candidate's own campaign; or to influence legislation, regulations, or policy debates. Most of the misinformation verbiage used in debates by candidates is political – either to attack an opponent or mischaracterize their own positions or accomplishments.

> **Negative Campaigning Happens Because It Works**
>
> Political campaigns often use misinformation in advertising and negative statements about opponents because they seem to work. For example, in the early 2000s, a national campaign leader responded to an interview question about an ad with clearly false Medicare information by saying it didn't matter because the ad "polls well."

---

3. For example, former U.S. Congressman George Santos (R-NY) apparently disseminated many fictional accounts of his life and accomplishments. https://www.vox.com/policy-and-politics/23520848/george-santos-fake-resume

4. One attempt to legitimize political misinformation was to label it as "alternative facts." https://theconversation.com/alternative-facts-do-exist-beliefs-lies-and-politics-84692

Election misinformation often focuses on claims that an election was "stolen." Spreaders of misinformation may assert that the voting process had been manipulated to create additional votes. They may accuse their opponents of hacking electronic voting machines, stuffing ballot boxes, or allowing non-citizens to vote. In 2024, as Vice President Harris was preparing to become the Democratic nominee, there was a dramatic increase in misinformation about elections.[5]

An example of election misinformation sprouting from a truth nugget is when a candidate is leading soon after the polls close on election day, but they end up with fewer votes when all the ballots have been counted. This reversal can be spun into misinformation that the election was rigged or stolen.

Truth Nuggets Behind Election & Political Misinformation

Just as misinformation about vaccines and COVID generally starts some nugget of truth – or truthiness – election and politic misinformation is often connected to a distant, immaterial fact.

An example of political misinformation was the claim that President Obama was not eligible to run for President because he was "not born in the U.S." The truth nuggets behind this were that Obama's father was born in Kenya, and he lived in Indonesia for a while when he was young. Even after Obama's U.S. birth status and citizenship were confirmed by the state of Hawaii, and in multiple court cases,[6] the misinformation persisted.

---

5. "Misinformation floods social media in wake of breakneck news cycle," The Hill, July 28, 2024 - https://thehill.com/policy/technology/4795180-misinformation-trump-biden-harris-2024/

6. https://en.wikipedia.org/wiki/Barack_Obama_citizenship_conspiracy_theories

People making those statements are seeking to change the results of an election by having certain votes discarded. They may challenge the validity of votes cast with early voting methods, such as absentee ballots or the use of drop boxes, or challenge the requirements for a person to document their citizenship or meet other requirements for registering to vote.

The candidate asserted that his opponent's brother was "a known homo sapien [sic]" and his sister was "a practicing thespian."[7]

• • •

Election misinformation generally has a shorter lifespan than political misinformation because it only has utility during the election cycle. The flames of election misinformation can be fanned for a while after the election if there are recounts or serious legal challenges. That misinformation can also be reused in subsequent elections to rally support and funding for a candidate.

However, fanning the flames of political misinformation can backfire. For example, the House of Representatives voted to repeal the Affordable Care Act so many times that many people assumed the law had actually been repealed. That may have reduced the value of the issue in subsequent campaigns.[8]

"Death Panels" in the Affordable Care Act

An example of mischaracterization of a legislative proposal occurred during the Congressional 2009 deliberations about the

---

7. This was reported to have been from a candidate in 1950 during a U.S. Senate primary election in Florida. https://www.gjsentinel.com/opinion/editorials/gumball-grading-highlights-pettiness-of-political-discourse/article_d2812b29-9459-5eef-98c5-a820d5f50a1b.html

8. The rise in the popularity of the ACA has also likely reduced the value of attacking it during campaigns. https://www.kff.org/affordable-care-act/poll-finding/5-charts-about-public-opinion-on-the-affordable-care-act/

> Affordable Care Act (ACA). The provision would have allowed Medicare to reimburse clinicians for end-of-life care consultations once every five years. The provision became controversial when it was labeled "Death Panels."[9] Because of the controversy, the provision was dropped,[10] but the impact stuck.[11] A few years after the ACA went into effect, many people – perhaps 30-40% – thought that the so-called "Death Panels" were part of the law.

Who is Spreading Misinformation about Elections

People and organizations create and spread misinformation about elections because they want to challenge or obscure the results. Their objective is to claim victory (and elected office) after they've lost an election.

Your friends' sources of misinformation about elections are likely different from their sources of misinformation about vaccines and COVID. But those sources' motivations are the same – **spreading misinformation for their own benefit or to create chaos and promote civil unrest.**[12] In contrast, altruistic spreaders[13] of misinformation may truly believe the candidate would be better for them and their community.

---

9. https://en.wikipedia.org/wiki/Death_panel & https://www.kff.org/from-drew-altman/what-death-panels-can-teach-us-about-health-misinformation/

10. Note: In 2016 Medicare began paying for that type of counseling. This was done through regulation rather than legislation, and "advance care planning" is covered as part of the Medicare Annual Wellness Visit. https://www.kff.org/medicare/fact-sheet/10-faqs-medicares-role-in-end-of-life-care/, and https://www.medicare.gov/coverage/advance-care-planning

11. https://read.dukeupress.edu/jhppl/article/40/5/1087/13766/The-Remarkable-Staying-Power-of-Death-Panels, and https://www.politico.com/magazine/story/2015/12/death-panels-obit-213481/

12. Those same organizations could be motivated to spread political misinformation in order to sway elections toward a candidate they believe would favor them if elected. This is sometimes referred to as "election interference."

13. See Chapter 2 for description of altruistic spreaders.

Winners of elections and their supporters have no reason to spread election misinformation.[14]

Why People May Be Susceptible to Election Misinformation

People who are susceptible to election misinformation might mistrust government organizations and get their information from sources with narrow perspectives.

If all your misinformed friend's neighbors, work colleagues and family voted for the candidate who lost, your friend may find it hard to understand how another candidate could have legitimately won. If they also heard misinformation about the election process from social media and politicians, that would strengthen their confidence that the election had been "stolen."

How to Talk with Friends Who are Misinformed about Elections

You can have productive discussions with friends who are misinformed about elections using the processes described in Chapter 2 and presented below. **Don't try to challenge your friend's facts**, as they likely believe that your facts are fictional. **Engage with them from a place of empathy**, and find out more about their emotions and personal motivations.

- **Your goal is not to convince them to switch allegiances to another party or candidate, but to reduce the friction in your relationship and loosen their grip on their misinformation about elections**
- Ask non-judgmental questions to understand their perspectives, motivations, and information sources

---

14. Sometimes stating the obvious helps illuminate a complicated landscape.

- Do not try and correct their misinformation with facts – that only leads to a "my facts v. your facts" argument

- You can use the Ask-Tell-Ask framework to introduce new perspectives from sources they trust and broaden the discussion by bringing in another person who they also trust

- If they divert the discussion away from the election process and want to talk about why their preferred candidate's policies are better, or the other candidate is "bad," then you need to shift the discussion back to the factual nature of elections

- If they assert false facts about the candidates, you may want to explore those by asking your friend non-judgmental questions, so you can understand their information sources and motivations

- If your friend associates their identity with the candidate's party and ideology, be careful to not engage in policy or moral discussions, and focus only on factual issues and misinformation

- Recognize that the process will involve a series of conversations – it won't be a one-shot discussion

Some examples of the things you can say during that process:

- "Can you tell me more about how you learned about the way the election was conducted?" *(Non-judgmental question – you are looking to understand them better)*

- "What do you think about our overall electoral process and how it affects our lives? *(Non-judgmental question that may give you insights about their sources of mistrust)*

- "It's great that you care so much about the election. That goes along with what I know about you being patriotic, and wanting a strong country and economy. What part of the election process troubles you the most?" *(Non-judgmental question that reinforces their rights to have concerns, which can help you begin the Ask-Tell-Ask process.)*

- If they steer the discussion toward their displeasure in the outcome of the election, then you need to redirect your discussion to the <u>process</u> of the election and away from the results. Examples of empathetic questions that will lead you there:

"A lot of people did vote for that person, but are their specific things about how the election was conducted that you are concerned about?"

"I understand that you don't like many of [**the other candidate's**] policy positions – and I fully support your right to disagree with those positions – but I'd like to talk more about **how the election itself was carried out**, since it is clearly still controversial. I would like to learn more about what you think about that. Would that be OK?" *(Non-judgmental questions redirecting discussion away from candidate's position or statements and back to the election.)*

- "Would it surprise you if [**name of trusted local political or community leader**] said there was no fraud in the election process?" *(Potential "Tell" part of the Ask-Tell-Ask process)*

Your friend may tell you that they mistrust what politicians say, yet quote those same politicians about how an election was "stolen" or "fraudulent." You may want to point out this logical conflict as part of an Ask-Tell-Ask process, but present it a way that is not overly challenging. For example:

- "You'd mentioned that you mistrust politicians and what they say – and I get that – but you also referred to politicians (or candidates) who claim that fraud occurred in the election or that it was stolen. What do you think about how those two things seem to be the opposite of each other? *(Tell and Ask part of the Ask-Tell-Ask process)*

If your friend doesn't appreciate the contradiction (or irony) that you've pointed out to them, then you should move on because it is likely you've created cognitive dissonance that is making them psychologically uncomfortable. You don't want to push them, or have an argument with them, which won't result in their suddenly having productive insights. The best you can hope for is that you may have planted a seed of doubt about politicians as a source of election (mis)information, and your friend will eventually accept that both things can't be correct, i.e., politicians can't be lying all the time while also being correct about election fraud.

- "It seems like **our country's enemies would benefit by encouraging people to question the validity of our elections.** That could disrupt the economy, which neither of us wants.[15] What do you think about that?" *(Potential follow-up question for the third part of the Ask-Tell-Ask process.)*

- "I appreciate your taking the time to share with me your perspectives about the election and the information you've gathered. It is clearly a complicated situation and I value our relationship. I'm glad we're able to talk about this in a civil way. Would it be OK for us to talk more about this again once I've had time to think more about what you said? And maybe we can include [name of trusted person] since I think they may have insights that neither of us have, which would be great to hear. Would that be OK?" *(Non-judgmental questions asking permission to continue the discussion and bring in a third person.)*

---

15. The 2024 Presidential election in Venezuela may be a case study of an attempt to steal an election.

> **Example of "Tell" Part of Ask-Tell-Ask for Election Misinformation**
>
> As mentioned in Chapter 2, someone – we'll call him "Bob" – used the Tell part of Ask-Tell-Ask to reduce friction in a relationship with a friend who insisted that the election had been stolen because their preferred candidate's lead in a major city disappeared overnight. Bob then checked with a former leader of the losing candidate's political party about whether the election in their state had been stolen. Bob reported back that the party leader had confirmed there was **no fraud** – the winning candidate's party had simply done a better job getting their supporters out to vote.

Remember, your tiered set of goals are to:

- **Reduce the friction in your relationships**
- **Decrease the spread of misinformation by helping people question their misinformation**
- **Loosen their grip on misinformation so they will question its validity and stop spreading it to others**

> **Agreeing on Goals Doesn't Mean Agreeing on Policies**
>
> People with different policy perspectives may agree on fundamental goals or outcomes, but strongly disagree about how to achieve those results. **To improve access to health care**, for example, some people favor building more hospitals and clinics. Other people want **to make insurance more affordable.** Some believe tax incentives are the best way to achieve that, while others favor direct payments, such as those in the Affordable Care Act. Those approaches have pros and cons, but none could be considered "incorrect."

When you are trying to move your friends away from misinformation, talk about factual misinformation rather than opinions, policy preferences or political ideologies. Election misinformation is about the election process and results. You don't want to talk with your friend about the pros and cons of the candidates or their policies – those are opinions and preferences, not facts.

If a friend or stranger **insists on talking about their policy perspectives** – and seems determined to focus on what is morally right and wrong – then you may not be able to have a motivation-based conversation with them. You should try to **redirect the conversation** to another topic to reduce the friction in your relationship.

<u>Talking with People Misinformed about Climate Change</u>

These section focuses on misinformation specific to the scientific data and facts about climate change.

We cannot conduct placebo-controlled trials to verify that climate change is occurring because of human activity. But the data shows that atmospheric carbon dioxide levels are rising, glaciers are melting, the frost season in northern and southern regions is growing shorter, and the natural ranges for plants, animals, and insects are shifting.

The nuggets of truth behind climate change misinformation are often things that can be observed or pointed to historically. Some examples of truth nuggets leading to assertions of misinformation are:

- Storms have always been bad, and it's very hard from personal observations to conclude that they've gotten worse – so climate change "can't be real"

- Weather patterns have changed over time, such as the dust bowl[16] drought in the 1920s in the U.S. – so any changes in climate are "natural" and not caused by anything people have done

- Seasons change from hot to cold and back again – so how can a change of a few degrees make a difference

- The tides go in and out – so an inch or two rise in sea levels "isn't significant"

> **Climate Change Has Consequences for Health and Economic Viability**
>
> A warming planet has consequences for human illness and the economic viability of towns and regions. For example, insects that carry diseases such as dengue fever are becoming established in new locations, and rising sea levels endanger the viability of coastal cities – or at least are requiring them to spend additional funds to preserve coastal roads and water systems. At higher latitudes, warming temperatures may be eliminating permafrost and extending growing seasons, enabling commercial agriculture in new locations.[17]

People who are susceptible to believing misinformation about climate change may have a strong sense of autonomy, which makes them more likely to believe only things that they can see themselves and mistrust experts. This makes them likely to oppose government mandates and actions.

---

16. https://drought.unl.edu/dustbowl/

17. https://climateandsecurity.org/2020/08/climate-change-in-russia-and-the-weaponization-of-wheat/ and https://www.nytimes.com/interactive/2020/12/16/magazine/russia-climate-migration-crisis.html

The susceptibility of people to climate change misinformation may depend on where they live, or how they make a living. People who work in agriculture may be less susceptible to climate change misinformation if they have seen the shift in the growing seasons, or the arrival of new plants and insects.

Climate change misinformation is actively spread for the same reasons as other types of misinformation – because spreaders of misinformation may benefit financially or may want to disrupt society. Industries that could be harmed by policies designed to limit climate change may have financial reasons to spread misinformation and to build opposition to those policies. They may characterize the science of climate change as a hoax,[18] in the same way the validity of COVID – and safety of vaccines – were questioned early in the pandemic.

You can have productive discussions with friends misinformed about climate change by using the approach you'd take if they were misinformed about elections, vaccines or COVID. Start by asking them non-judgmental questions about their perspectives and concerns. You don't want to challenge them with facts and figures about things like average temperatures and atmospheric CO_2 levels. Some friends may be concerned about the economic effects of reducing the use of fossil fuels. Others may object to government "mandates" about what type of cars and light bulbs[19] can be sold, or how electricity is produced.

---

18. https://climate.law.columbia.edu/content/climate-change-described-hoax-louisiana-attorney-general-0 and https://www.tandfonline.com/doi/full/10.1080/23251042.2020.1855884

19. "Phase-out of incandescent bulbs," Wikipedia (Accesses 10/10/24) https://en.wikipedia.org/wiki/Phase-out_of_incandescent_light_bulbs, "Debunking Myths about Phasing Out the Incandescent Lightbulb," Department of Energy 8/11/23 (Accessed 10/10/24) https://www.energy.gov/articles/debunking-myths-about-phasing-out-incandescent-lightbulb, and "Why Republicans are fighting to save the 30-cent light bulb," Christian Science Monitor, 7/11/2011 https://www.csmonitor.com/USA/Politics/2011/0711/Why-Republicans-are-fighting-to-save-the-30-cent-light-bulb

Your next step is to talk with your friend to understand their motivations, which could include:

- They want to maintain the town's economic growth, which may depend on agriculture or tourism[20]

- They are farmers who want to pass along their productive farmland to their children

- They prioritize national security, so they don't want responses to climate change to economically disadvantage the country or reduce the nation's energy independence

> **Secondary Benefits of Policies Responding to Climate Change**
>
> Economic growth and national security can improve if the government takes specific action to slow climate change: encouraging reforestation, developing new energy sources, promoting electric vehicles, and stabilizing coastlines.

Someone who is misinformed about climate change could be very judgmental if you don't agree with them. In that situation, use the options described in Chapter 3 for disengaging or changing the topic to something non-controversial, like a local sports teams.

Summary & Conclusions

- **You can help your misinformed friends** question their misinformation about the election process and climate change, and travel a path to rejecting their misinformation.

---

20. Tourist locations based in coastal areas may be threatened by rising sea levels, and mountain locations may have their tourism threatened by reduced snowfall, or increased rain leading to flooding.

- Having these conversations will **reduce the friction in your relationships** and lead misinformed people to loosen their grip on misinformation. This will make them less likely to spread the misinformation.

- You want your discussions to **build on your mutual trust** – don't antagonize your friend by challenging their "facts."

- **Listen actively and ask non-judgmental questions** whenever you're talking with a misinformed friend, co-worker or family member. Focus on their motivations, such as a strong economy and country, so you can move the conversation down a better path over time.

- You can use the **Ask-Tell-Ask process** to help someone consider new perspectives by bringing new insights from people they trust into the discussion.

- **Your friends' perspectives are not going to change rapidly**. You will need to engage with your friend, family member or co-worker multiple times, with each discussion building on your previous conversations.

- Your discussions can be more effective – and faster – if you bring in other friends who are **trusted allies** to reinforce your non-judgmental questions and expand the conversations.

- If a misinformed friend tries to try to convince you that their preferred candidate is better qualified, **guide the conversation back to the election process** and away from the candidates' policies and your friend's political preferences.

- When misinformation arises in a group setting, **you want to avoid getting into a "my facts v. your facts argument,"** which could happen if someone in the group tries to correct the misinformation with facts. You may be able to **defuse the tension** by changing the topic. If the person who brought up the misinformation is a friend, try to arrange a one-on-one conversation with them at another time.

- If you find yourself in a discussion about elections or climate change with a stranger, **consider your safety first**. If you can disengage, that may be your best option. If you cannot disengage, try to change the topic to something non-controversial.

- If election or climate change misinformation arises in a community conversation – in a newspaper, on a local social media platform like Facebook, or at a Town Council meeting – you should use the techniques for reversing misinformation described in Chapter 4.

Notes: Election or Climate Change Misinformation

My misinformed friends, family or co-workers _____

Specific aspects of the election (or climate change) that [Person #1] is misinformed about
_____

Major Reasons [Person #1] is Misinformed about an Election/Climate Change
_____

- Mistrust about X, Y, Z _____
- Historical or family experience _____
- Feeling that their autonomy is threatened by _____

Non-judgmental questions to ask [Person #1] ("Can you tell me more about that?")
_____

<u>Ask > Tell > Ask Process:</u>
- Ask permission to talk about _____
- Tell information in a non-judgmental way as a question;
  "Would it surprise you to hear that [Another Respected Person] said
  _____?"

- Ask follow-up questions to guide your discussion back to the misinformation

Mutual friends/trusted allies you can enlist to reinforce your questions and discussions
_____

- Thank you for sharing your insights with me.
- I'd really like to continue our discussion soon. Would that be OK?
- I'd like to bring in [Trusted Ally] to talk about this with us. Would that be all right with you?

Chapter 6

Social Media & Misinformation

"Living is easy with eyes closed, misunderstanding all you see."[1]

This chapter is about how you can **work with your friends and community to help prevent misinformation from spreading through social media platforms.** Misinformation on social media can be about vaccines, serious illnesses like COVID, elections, climate change, natural disasters,[2] government actions,[3] and people, especially celebrities.

---

1. Lyrics from the song Strawberry Fields by John Lennon (1967)

2. https://www.politico.com/newsletters/weekly-cybersecurity/2023/09/11/influence-campaign-spread-during-maui-wildfires-00114944, and https://www.mediamatters.org/hurricanes/hurricane-milton-grows-so-do-conspiracy-theories-falsely-attributing-hurricanes-weather

3. "FEMA chief decries rumors, disinformation about hurricane recovery as worst ever," 10/8/2024 https://alabamareflector.com/2024/10/08/fema-chief-decries-rumors-disinformation-about-hurricane-recovery-as-worst-ever/, and "Bizarre Falsehoods About Hurricanes Helene and Milton Disrupt Recovery Efforts," 10/10/2024 https://www.nytimes.com/2024/10/10/business/media/hurricane-milton-helene-conspiracy-theories.html

Prebunking is the broad term for teaching people to recognize misinformation – it makes people less likely to believe misinformation when they see it. You can help your friends and people in your community become more resistant to misinformation on social media with prebunking and by improving media literacy. (Note that working with friends and people in your community is easier than trying to influence the actions of private companies or to change federal laws regulating social media companies.)

What is Social Media?

For the purposes of this chapter, "social media" are platforms that present content in the form of text, video or audio where users can comment on, react to or share the content. The audience typically has the opportunity to leave a comment, "Like" the content, or share it with others on that platform.[4] Applications on our phones that enable exchanging, sharing and commenting on information are also a form of social media. In Mr. Magoo's hypothetical blog, YouTube channel, and podcast,[5] for example, Mr. Magoo would be presenting the content, and all the people "tuning in" would be his audience.

Social Media is different from traditional media, which transmits information via TV channels and physical publications. Importantly, **the FCC regulates traditional broadcast media** and can hold them accountable for incorrect information and defamation. **Physical publications** are subject to similar laws. **In contrast, social media is protected from that type of legal and regulatory accountability by Section 230 of the Federal Communications Act.**

---

4. News websites often have similar capabilities, and often allow their audience to share links to the content on multiple social media platforms.

5. Mr. Magoo was a fictional cartoon character created in the late 1940s. Wearing very thick glasses (because he was extremely myopic) was one of his key characteristics. Another was his refusing to admit the existence of any problems – many of which were caused by his poor eyesight. https://en.wikipedia.org/wiki/Mr._Magoo The copyright to the character seems to be currently owned by DreamWorks Classics, a division of Comcast. https://en.wikipedia.org/wiki/United_Productions_of_America

Social media platforms include Facebook, YouTube, Reddit, Twitter/X, Bluesky, Threads, Mastodon, Instagram, LinkedIn, TruthSocial, NextDoor, Pinterest, TikTok, SnapChat, and the vast number of blogs hosted all over the place.

Discussions on different platforms differ in terms of tenor and culture. LinkedIn is designed for people interested in business, and Reddit is for people who want to ask questions or share information in specific subreddits.[6] Twitter/X is often more biting. NextDoor typically helps people learn about local resources and community events.

Every social media platform has a particular appeal to its intended audience. Snapchat and TikTok skew towards younger users, Facebook skews toward older users, and Pinterest users are predominantly women.[7] Marketing companies rely on each social media platforms' user demographics to target ads and content to likely customers.[8] Political and advocacy organizations do this, too.

Young People are Getting News from Social Media

Young people used to get a lot of their news and information from TV shows like "The Daily Show with Jon Stewart,"[9] which is subject to FCC scrutiny for incorrect or defamatory material. Now, young people are reportedly getting more of their news and information

---

6. https://support.reddithelp.com/hc/en-us/articles/204533569-What-are-communities-or-subreddits

7. https://www.pewresearch.org/internet/fact-sheet/social-media/?tabItem=5b319c90-7363-4881-8e6f-f98925683a2f and https://sproutsocial.com/insights/new-social-media-demographics/ (Accessed 9/29/24)

8. https://khoros.com/resources/social-media-demographics-guide

9. "Young Get News from Comedy Central," CBS News, March 1, 2004 https://www.cbsnews.com/news/young-get-news-from-comedy-central/

> from social media,[10] which is not subject to that FCC oversight because of Section 230 of the Federal Communications Act.

It is not unreasonable to view social media as an infinite series of cesspools with a few interspersed fertile ponds.

The power of social media is difficult to measure, as it is a constantly changing landscape of niche information sources. Instagram began with pictures and then added video. Twitter (now X) used to limit its content to 140 characters before extending that to 280 characters, then 4,000 or more for Premium subscribers.[11] Many social media platforms that are popular today didn't exist years ago. Some older sites like Myspace have fallen out of favor,[12] and many blogs have come and gone or become dormant.

How Social Media Platforms Operate

Every social media platform or company has its own algorithms and policies, and moderates content in its own way.

Purveyors of misinformation – like legitimate advertisers – spread their "brand" strategically. They target specific groups of people via their targets' favorite social media platform.

Many social media platforms use algorithms that preferentially boost what is more emotionally engaging – which often means content that riles people up or makes them angry. Spreaders of

---

10. "More Americans – especially young adults – are regularly getting news on TikTok," Pew Research Center, September 17, 2024 https://www.pewresearch.org/short-reads/2024/09/17/more-americans-regularly-get-news-on-tiktok-especially-young-adults/ (Accessed October 9, 2024)

11. https://www.forbes.com/sites/nicholasreimann/2023/02/08/twitter-boosts-character-limit-to-4000-for-twitter-blue-subscribers/, and https://circleboom.com/blog/how-to-tweet-more-than-280-characters-on-twitter/

12. https://em360tech.com/tech-article/what-happened-to-myspace

misinformation leverage the algorithms' preference for negative content when they generate misinformation. That is why you're unlikely to see misinformation that says something like "If you click your heels together three times every day, you'll be a better, kinder person."

A seemingly benign piece of misinformation that circles constantly on Facebook is that you can see more of your friends' posts by copying and pasting a particular block of text into your feed.[13] This annoying trope stays alive because if feeds off people's anger or fear that somehow Facebook's algorithms are keeping them from seeing things from their friends. (Why would Facebook want to do that? Wouldn't that defeat the purpose of Facebook, which wants you to keep you scrolling so you see more ads?)

Does That Seem Right?

I've suggested to people that they look at the Snopes website[14] to verify whether something is true or a hoax. For some people that works. In the future, they may remember to "do more research" and look at Snopes of other reliable debunking websites. (See the end of this chapter for other resources.) People can develop good instincts about misinformation: **if something sounds too good to be true, then It. Usually. Is. Not. True.**

<u>Preventing Your Friends and Community from Being Infected with Misinformation on Social Media</u>

Preventing people you know – and others in your community – from absorbing misinformation from social media is a challenging task. **Improving people's media literacy and pre-bunking training** can make people more resistant to being infected with misinformation, as

---

13. https://www.snopes.com/fact-check/facebook-bypass-system-hoax/

14. www.snopes.com

described in Chapter 4.

> **Learn More about Media Literacy**
>
> Media Literacy Now is a non-profit organization that focuses on "policy change at local, state, and national levels in the U.S. to ensure all K-12 students are taught media literacy so that they become healthy, confident and competent media consumers and creators."[15] Many other organizations and resources also focus on media literacy.[16] (Also see Chapter 4.)

The key is to get your friends to question what they see on the internet or their phone Apps. Unfortunately, there isn't a switch you can pull, a patch you can place, or a pill or a shot that will make your friends – or people in your community – resistant to misinformation on social media.

Providing Insight into Social Media Ads and Suggestions

The major social media platforms suggest content and present ads for you engage with that are similar to what you've previously liked, shared or commented on. Those suggestions are created by the social media platform's algorithms, working to provide you with the experience they think you will want – which will benefit their paying customers and advertisers.

If you want help a friend who is receptive to misinformation, one tactic you can try is to point out that the **ads and "suggestions" on social media are not random** – and not necessarily harmless. This may work best if your conversations are already going well, and your

---

15. https://medialiteracynow.org/about/mission/

16. See places listed here: https://thetrustedweb.org/organizations-leading-the-fight-against-fake-news/

friend is beginning to question misinformation on social media. You might use the Ask-Tell-Ask process to present the idea that social media algorithms are showing them manipulative ads and suggestions. But be mindful of timing. If it's too early in your discussions, your insight may seem judgmental or coercive. **You always want to meet the other person where they are, and not try to drag them to where you are.**

Vote with Your Eyeballs and Screen Time

As a user of social media, you have the option to "vote with your eyeballs" by deleting your account on any social media platforms that you think are promoting misinformation. If your company or organization uses social media channels, you may be in a position to choose which platforms it uses – and does not use.[17]

Controlling Misinformation on Social Media

Social media platforms use their own guidelines, governing laws, and regulations to determine what type of content is objectionable. They use various processes for identifying unacceptable content, a practice known as "moderation" or "moderating content."

As they try to moderate content, social media platforms use algorithms to screen for certain characteristics of the text or images, which can then be reviewed by actual humans. Many platforms also allow users to block what they see from other users, and from others seeing or commenting on what they've posted. Some platforms also permit users to flag or report content that they believe is objectionable or against

---

17. An executive I know at a print publication – which of course has a website and significant social media presence – is considering deleting one of the publication's social media accounts because of the amount of misinformation spreading on that platform.

the platform's rules.[18] In theory, flagged content will be reviewed by a human being, and potentially removed by the platform.

Every social media platform has different rules for what they deem unacceptable, and how they carry out their moderating process. For example, Pinterest does not allow misinformation about vaccines.[19] That is a decision the company made back in 2019, but they seem to be the only social media platform to have made that commitment.

The effectiveness of each platform's moderation can be debated, although personal experience is instructive. If you have flagged or reported content on social media platforms – as I have – you may have found the process unsatisfactory. The one type of content that platforms seem to do a better job of removing when notified by individuals is copyright-protected material.

Why Social Media is Such a Hard-to-Control Mess

U.S. social media companies are generally not responsible for misinformation posted by users on their platforms because of Section 230 of the Federal Communications Act.[20] Section 230 was created in 1996 and says that social media companies are not responsible for what their users post on their platforms, with some limited exceptions such as copyrighted material or material that violates

---

18. How to report misinformation to social media platforms so they (might) take it down can be found here: https://counterhate.com/blog/how-to-report-misinformation-on-social-media/

19. Pinterest's policy states "Pinterest's misinformation policy prohibits things like promotion of false cures for terminal or chronic illnesses and anti-vaccination advice." https://help.pinterest.com/en/article/health-misinformation (Accessed June 10, 2024)

20. "Understanding Section 230 – Social Media Companies' Get Out of Jail Free Card," May 17, 2024 - https://counterhate.com/blog/understanding-section-230-social-media-companies-get-out-of-jail-free-card/, "These 26 words 'created the internet.' Now the Supreme Court may be coming for them," 2/18/2023 https://www.cnn.com/2023/02/18/tech/section-230-explainer/index.html, "Section 230: An Overview," Congressional Research Service (Published 5/3/2023 and Updated 1/4/2024), https://crsreports.congress.gov/product/pdf/R/R46751,

federal criminal law.

Social media companies wanted the protections in Section 230. They were concerned that without those protections they would face lawsuits that would prevent them from becoming viable businesses, which would undermine their ability to grow in the U.S.

Section 230's legal protections recognized that social media platforms are different from newspapers or broadcast news, which have limited space or time to present material to their audiences. In contrast, social media's breadth is limitless. Newspapers and TV networks choose the articles and opinion pieces they publish. Social media platforms do not choose what their users publish. In theory, anyone can have their own YouTube channel and Instagram feed to post videos of whatever they want, from cats playing, to a person sitting behind a desk with logos of their "news" show about aliens, the occult, gardening, auto repair, or vaccines. ("Fun With Flags presented by Sheldon Cooper" was a fictional on-line show from the actual TV show "The Big Bang Theory." Clips from those episodes are – of course – on YouTube.[21])

Other countries and regions have their own laws, rules and oversight processes, such as the E.U.'s Digital Services Act,[22] created to prevent "illegal and harmful activities online and the spread of misinformation." Brazil recently got into a spat with X (formerly Twitter) about misinformation. As the Washington Post reported, "Supreme Court Justice Alexandre de Moraes, who oversees Brazil's inquiry into fake news, had asked the platform to suspend accounts he accused of spreading disinformation that he said could harm the country's democratic instit

---

21. https://www.youtube.com/watch?v=hjzRbgxZXz8

22. https://commission.europa.eu/strategy-and-policy/priorities-2019-2024/europe-fit-digital-age/digital-services-act_en

utions."²³ After much legal back and forth, Brazil suspended X until the company agreed to comply with Brazilian law.

• • •

While a full discussion of free speech protection and the intricacies of international communications laws are beyond the scope of this book, here are potential guardrails for limiting misinformation on social media in the U.S.

Changing Section 230 of the Federal Communications Act

Because Section 230 is central to how social media platforms operate in the U.S., legislation has been proposed that would make social media companies responsible for false information on their platforms.

Thirty years ago, it seemed logistically impossible for the companies hosting chat rooms and providing internet access to moderate content. Today, content moderation is still difficult, but it can be done. Some companies do a much better job than others, and others seem to not do much at all. Twitter/X, for example, reportedly cut their moderation department dramatically and has allowed individuals who were previously banned from the platform for posting misinformation to reactivate accounts or create new ones.²⁴

Although – as an individual – you are unlikely to be able to change Federal law, you can add your voice to those calling for social media

---

23. "Judge lifts suspension of X in Brazil after it meets court's demands," Washington Post, 10/8/2024 https://www.washingtonpost.com/world/2024/10/08/brazilian-judge-lifts-suspension-x-after-it-cedes-courts-demands/ (Accessed 10/9/24)

24. "The mass unbanning of suspended Twitter users is underway," CNN.com December 8, 2022, https://www.cnn.com/2022/12/08/tech/twitter-unbanned-users-returning/index.html, "Twitter's Moderation System Is in Tatters," Wired, November 17, 2022 https://www.wired.com/story/twitters-moderation-system-is-in-tatters/, and "Twitter Fires Election Integrity Team Ahead of 2024 Elections," Rolling Stoner, September 27, 2023 https://www.rollingstone.com/culture/culture-news/twitter-elon-musk-fires-safety-team-2024-elections-1234832199/ (Accessed October 9, 2024)

companies to be held responsible for the content they allow. You can contact your Members of Congress or the relevant regulatory agencies like the FCC. Your message should be that social media companies should be responsible for all the information on their platforms, and for conducting meaningful and timely moderation of their content. You can write to your Members of Congress,[25] attend their Town Hall Meetings and ask questions/make statements. You can talk with their staff people, who tend to be very good (though busy).

Of course, even if new laws are passed to make social media companies responsible for the content on their platforms, it will likely lead to lengthy litigation. But everything is not hopeless. The Senate passed the Kids Online Safety Act with major bipartisan support.[26] And some states[27] have passed laws, although they will likely face legal challenges.

Another option for controlling misinformation on social media would be to **create a new Federal agency** (or expand the authority of an existing agency) **to monitor and regulate commercial speech that is harming people.** This approach would be similar to how the FDA regulates commercial communications about medical products, such as product labelling, consumer advertising, and even the names of pharmaceuticals products.[28]

---

25. You can find your Member of Congress here: https://www.congress.gov/members/find-your-member Each member has a website with information about how to contact them.

26. "Senate passes the most significant child online safety bills in decades," July 30, 2024 (Accessed 11/3/2024) https://www.nbcnews.com/politics/congress/senate-poised-pass-significant-child-online-safety-bills-decades-rcna164259

27. "Newsom Signs Bill That Adds Protections for Children on Social Media," The New York Times, September 21, 2024 https://www.nytimes.com/2024/09/21/us/newsom-children-social-media-bill.html (Accessed 10/9/24)

28. Most people don't realize that the FDA has to approve the names of medicines. For example, a new medicine to treat cancer most certainly couldn't be named "Cancer-Be-Gone." This is not an infringement on the pharmaceutical company's first amendment rights since this is commercial "speech" rather than personal speech.

Warning About Challenging or Correcting Misinformation on Social Media

While you may be tempted to correct or challenge misinformation that you see on social media, please be very, very careful. Because social media platforms are often open systems where people from all over the world can see what you've posted, you are putting yourself out there as a potential target. Unfortunately, while the internet is virtual, there are people and organizations that may **flame** you online, and more importantly, they may bring their anger and vitriol into the real world by directly or indirectly encourage **doxing** or **swatting**.

- **Flaming** is when someone posts nasty things about you online to try and ruin your reputation. If you have a business presence on the internet, they may post very negative reviews and recruit others to do the same.

- **Doxing** is when someone posts your physical address and other information (such as phone number, date of birth, or social security number) and encourages others to attack you or steal your identity.

- **Swatting** is when someone spoofs[29] your home phone number and places a call to the local police claiming that something horrible is going on – such as an armed home invasion. This may result in a rapid, armed response from the police.

These scenarios are not just fantasies. There has been at least one case where the person being swatted was killed by the police. During the height of the COVID pandemic, clinical and scientific experts who tried to refute misinformation about vaccines and COVID were virtually and physically harassed and confronted in very unpleasant ways.

---

29. According to the FCC, "Caller ID spoofing is when a caller deliberately falsifies the information transmitted to your caller ID display to disguise their identity." https://www.fcc.gov/spoofing#

Realistically, if you occasionally push back by saying something like "That doesn't sound right," you're unlikely to be targeted by not-nice-people, but you need to evaluate the risks and benefits of your online actions.

Just to repeat, please be careful if you engage with people on social media. Even people you know could repost your comments and include a link to your profile. Please follow the adage from Chapter 4: **"Don't wrestle with pigs. You both get dirty, and the pigs like it."**

Additional Resources

The goal of this chapter was to give you an overview of the rapidly-evolving landscape of misinformation on social media, and suggest possible actions. Although your opportunities for changing misinformation on social media may be limited, listed below are some organizations where you can find additional insights about misinformation. Some of these organizations may provide suggestions for how you might prevent misinformation from taking hold or spreading on social media.

- The Center for Countering Digital Hate[30] https://counterhate.com/

- www.Snopes.com

- FactCheck.org – A Project of the Annenberg Public Policy Center at the University of Pennsylvania https://www.factcheck.org/ Also see SciCheck, which focuses on "false and misleading scientific claims that are made by partisans to influence public policy" https://www.factcheck.org/scicheck/

- PolitiFact at The Poynter Institute https://www.politifact.com/

---

30. Note: The owner of the social media platform X (formerly Twitter) is reportedly engaged in significant legal action against CCDH because of CCDH's articles about misinformation being spread on X. https://www.npr.org/2023/08/01/1191318468/elon-musk-sues-disinformation-researchers-claiming-they-are-driving-away-adverti, and https://www.reuters.com/technology/musks-x-corp-loses-lawsuit-against-hate-speech-watchdog-2024-03-25/

Summary & Conclusions

The chaos of misinformation on social media may seem depressing because it sprouts so easily and spreads rapidly across platforms. But I believe there is hope. Social media companies can restrict or ban misinformation if they want to (as Pinterest did in 2019). And some policymakers are talking about the problem, even if the likelihood of legislative changes seems low at the moment.

While it is unlikely that other social media platforms will voluntarily follow Pinterest's example, there are some things you can consider doing to minimize the influence of misinformation on social media. And there are certain things you should be cautious about.

- **You can support improving media literacy in your community** by talking with your friends and family about media literacy, and having substantive discussions with the leadership of your schools and city/county governments. You can also make statements at public meetings of organizations like the PTA and Town Council about the dangers of misinformation, and what the local community can do to address it by improving media literacy. (See more about this in Chapter 4.)

- **You can help educate children and adults about the scientific method, critical thinking, and media literacy** – particularly about how to discern valid media sources from those that are spreading misinformation. This will raise their awareness about the harms being caused by misinformation on social media, and help prevent misinformation from taking root.

- You can **talk with your elected officials** – particularly Members of Congress and Governors (and their staffs) – who are increasingly aware of the problem of misinformation on social media. Your support for their efforts would motivate them potentially to take legislative or regulatory action.

- **Be careful what you do on social media to refute or correct misinformation.** Interacting with misinformed people on social media is very different from having productive conversations in in the physical world. You do not know strangers' history or motivations, and they may take actions remotely that could harm you, such as Flaming, Doxing or Swatting. Since your safety is your first priority, be careful about trying to refute misinformation on social media.

Chapter 7

Artificial Intelligence & Misinformation

In theory it's all practical, but in practice it's all theoretical.[1]

This chapter gives you an overview of how AI systems are **affecting the creation and spread of misinformation.**

Be aware – the landscape of AI systems is shifting very rapidly. What is in this chapter could be out of date by the middle of 2025.

Some people believe that artificial intelligence will make it easier to identify and contain misinformation. Unfortunately, AI system also makes misinformation easier and less expensive to create and share. My fear is that while AIs can do both, they will be used increasingly to infect people with misinformation.

---

1. Albert Einstein reportedly said "In theory, theory and practice are the same. In practice, they are not," Immanuel Kant reportedly said "Theory without practice is empty; practice without theory is blind," and Yogi Berra – perhaps one of the greatest modern philosophers and creators of tortured English prose – reportedly said, "In theory there is no difference between theory and practice - in practice there is."

Understanding the mutating matrix of AI systems will give you insights into how AI is shaping your misinformed friends' views and actions. As you advocate for more media literacy education and resources in your community, it will be useful to know how AI is worsening the misinformation problem.

As individuals, there is not much we can do to influence the development and use of AI systems.

> ### What is AI?
>
> AI started with static algorithms that were refined over time to improve their effectiveness and accuracy. In medicine, for example, those types of algorithms have been used for decades to analyze EKGs[2] and scan PAP smears for abnormal cells.[3]
>
> Newer AI systems are capable of continuously incorporating data, and can modify their programming or algorithms to provide better information. Those AI systems may be called "machine learning" or MLAI.[4]
>
> Some AI systems not only analyze data and learn from it – they can also create something new or novel. In the consumer world, ChatGPT and its relatives generate new content and images quickly. That output can be used for social media and press releases, academic papers, and legal briefs.
>
> One potential risk of AI systems that update themselves continuously is that incorporating lower-quality data may result in worse

---

2. https://www.tandfonline.com/doi/abs/10.3109/14639238909010878

3. https://pubmed.ncbi.nlm.nih.gov/8621186/

4. This type of MLAI is also sometimes referred to as "adaptive" since it is continually adapting to new data and information it encounters.

> output.[5] This has been termed "model contamination via feedback loops."[6]

Will AI Be Good or Bad for Misinformation?

AI systems are only as useful as the data used to create them, and the data they're fed as they grow. Although AI systems may learn from extremely large datasets, if those datasets are biased or skewed – either intentionally or unintentionally – the results they deliver may be misleading or completely wrong.

AI systems can be used for nefarious purposes. For example, they can create "deep fake" videos and audios, including voices. False AI-generated content about candidates, election processes, natural disasters or celebrities can be used to influence voters, or scare people into buying things. It can send people on social media to websites that are riddled with malware or engineered to steal their money or identity.

False audio is already being used by telemarketers (both legitimate and scammers) to lure people into speaking with a live person. Even more alarmingly, fraudsters are impersonating people with AI-generated audio, to scam their relatives out of money. This is the next generation of the "Grandparent Scam." (See below.)

---

5. Government Accountability Office. (2022, November 10). Artificial Intelligence in Health Care: Benefits and Challenges of Machine Learning Technologies for Medical Diagnostics. https://www.gao.gov/products/gao-22-104629

6. "Feedback Loops and Model Contamination: The AI Ouroboros Crisis," August 24, 2024 (Accessed 10-14-2024) https://sease.io/2024/08/feedback-loops-and-model-contamination-the-ai-ouroboros-crisis.html

Grandparent Scam Enhanced by AI

The following text from the Federal Communications Commission[7] describes how scammers are using AI to impersonate grandchildren, so they can steal money from unsuspecting elderly people. This scam originated with real people pretending to be the grandchild on a phone call. Now the AI creates the voices to make the "call for help" more convincing.

"Scammers who gain access to consumers' personal information – by mining social media or purchasing data from cyber thieves – can create storylines to prey on the fears of grandparents. The scammers call and impersonate a grandchild – or another close relative – in a crisis situation, asking for immediate financial assistance. Sometimes these callers "spoof" the caller ID to make an incoming call appear to be coming from a trusted source."

"Often the imposter claims to have been in an accident or arrested. The scammer may ask the grandparent "please don't let mom and dad know," and may hand the phone over to someone posing as a lawyer seeking immediate payment."

"Unfortunately, bad actors can now use artificial intelligence technology, commonly known as AI, and a short audio or video clip to "clone" a loved one's voice, according to the Federal Trade Commission."[8]

---

7. "'Grandparent' Scams Get More Sophisticated," Updated Feb. 1, 2024," (Accessed 10/16/24) https://www.fcc.gov/grandparent-scams-get-more-sophisticated

8. "Scammers use AI to enhance their family emergency schemes," March 23, 2023 (Accessed 10/16/2024) https://consumer.ftc.gov/consumer-alerts/2023/03/scammers-use-ai-enhance-their-family-emergency-schemes

Because of concerns about how quickly AI is evolving and how broadly it is being used, government regulators and policymakers are trying to manage the creation and use of AI systems.

In 2019, the U.S. government created an AI website[9] that was initially focused on promoting AI as a competitive technology, but is now much broader in scope.[10] Since 2019, there have been legislative hearings,[11] and a U.S. Presidential Executive Order establishing a Task Force within the Department of Health and Human Services to create an AI strategic plan.[12]

The Executive Order's health care provisions built upon previous actions, including:

- "Voluntary commitments from 15 leading companies to drive safe, secure, and trustworthy development of AI"[13]

- The Administration's "Blueprint for an AI Bill of Rights"[14]

---

9. https://web.archive.org/web/20190319183107/https://www.whitehouse.gov/ai/executive-order-ai/

10. https://ai.gov/

11. https://www.brookings.edu/articles/senate-hearing-highlights-ai-harms-and-need-for-tougher-regulation/, and https://www.c-span.org/video/?530327-1/hearingon-regulatingartificial-intelligence#

12. https://www.whitehouse.gov/briefing-room/presidential-actions/2023/10/30/executive-order-on-the-safe-secure-and-trustworthy-development-and-use-of-artificial-intelligence/

13. https://www.whitehouse.gov/briefing-room/statements-releases/2023/10/30/fact-sheet-president-biden-issues-executive-order-on-safe-secure-and-trustworthy-artificial-intelligence/

14. https://www.whitehouse.gov/ostp/ai-bill-of-rights/

- The previous Executive Order to combat discrimination that includes provisions concerning AI[15]

- Ongoing activities by the FDA related to AI[16]

Since the government is exploring ways to regulate AI, you may be able to advocate for regulations that would limit the spread of misinformation. Contact your elected officials or people at the regulatory agencies like the FCC to express your concerns about how AI systems are making misinformation worse, particularly related to public health, disaster relief, and elections.

How AI Systems View Their Ability to Prevent or Spread Misinformation

To understand how AI systems might increase or prevent the spread and harms caused by misinformation, I went to some "experts." A friend of mine asked five publicly-available AI systems[17] the following questions:

"How will A.I. prevent the spread and creation of misinformation (particularly with vaccines and elections)? How might A.I. increase the spread? Please provide references where necessary."[18]

---

15. https://www.whitehouse.gov/briefing-room/presidential-actions/2021/01/20/executive-order-advancing-racial-equity-and-support-for-underserved-communities-through-the-federal-government/

16. https://www.fda.gov/news-events/press-announcements/fda-releases-artificial-intelligencemachine-learning-action-plan, https://www.fda.gov/regulatory-information/search-fda-guidance-documents/marketing-submission-recommendations-predetermined-change-control-plan-artificial, and https://www.mintz.com/insights-center/viewpoints/2791/2021-10-04-coverage-fdas-aiml-medical-devices-workshop-part-1

17. Chat GPT4o, Claude 3.5 Sonnet, Gemini 1.5 with Flash, MS Copilot, and perplexity.ai, (accessed October 10, 2024)

18. These queries could have gone into greater detail by asking the AIs to compare their findings about how to prevent or spread misinformation to what other AIs recommended. But because AI evolves so fast, the answers would quickly have become outdated.

Not surprisingly, all five AI systems gave similar responses, which I've summarized and quoted below.

AI systems can <u>prevent</u> the spread of misinformation by:

- **Detecting Misinformation.** AIs can be used by individuals, content moderators or other AIs to "fact check" information and determine its validity. One of the AI systems stated that AIs can be trained to detect deepfake videos.

- **Moderating Content.** AI systems can automatically screen on-line and social media and other online content for misinformation.

- **Tracking and Predicting Misinformation.** By analyzing metadata and users' behaviors, AI systems can predict which on-line sources appear to be generating misinformation and are likely to create misinformation in the future.

- **Helping Human Fact-Checkers.** AI systems can support human fact-checkers at traditional news media companies. That type of assistance can be particularly useful during fast-moving events like elections and public emergencies (like infectious disease outbreaks, weather events and earthquakes).

- **Validating Content for Social Media Users.** AI systems can help social media users determine – in near real time – the validity of content being posted by other users.

However, AI systems can also <u>increase</u> the spread of misinformation by:

- **Creating Deepfakes and Other Synthetic Media.** AI systems can create highly convincing fake videos, images, and audio, making it harder to distinguish real from fabricated content, as in the Grandparent Scam above.

- **Amplifying the Spread of Misinformation with Algorithms. "AI algorithms may **inadvertently** promote sensational or divisive content, including misinformation." [Emphasis added] AI systems can target that misinformation to individuals: "AI algorithms can analyze user data to create highly targeted misinformation campaigns, tailoring content to specific individuals or groups for maximum impact."

- **Creating Echo Chambers on Social Media.** AI systems can use algorithms to feed social media users more of the types of misinformation they have already engaged with, which reinforces their belief in the misinformation. One AI system called this **"Personalized Propaganda."**

- **Directly Spreading Misinformation.** If AI systems use misinformation and treat it as accurate, they can contribute to the spread of misinformation. As one AI system responded, **"Generative AI systems can unintentionally spread misinformation** when users generate content that presents false or misleading information. While such tools are intended for generating helpful or accurate responses, they can be manipulated to produce and disseminate false information, particularly when used in bad faith." Another AI system noted that **"Bad actors could exploit vulnerabilities in AI systems to manipulate their outputs or training data."**

Conclusions from the five AI systems included:

- "AI has immense potential to reduce the spread of misinformation, but it requires responsible deployment."

- "AI has the potential to both help prevent and increase the spread of misinformation, particularly regarding sensitive topics like vaccines and elections."

- "The effectiveness of AI in combating or spreading misinformation depends greatly on how it is developed, deployed, and regulated."

- "The effectiveness of AI in preventing or spreading misinformation depends on how it is developed and deployed. **It is essential to ensure that AI is used ethically and responsibly to combat the spread of false information.**"

- One AI system presented a set of recommendations titled "Balancing AI's Impact."

"To leverage AI's potential for combating misinformation while mitigating its risks, a multi-faceted approach is necessary:

1. Developing **robust AI detection systems** to identify and flag potential misinformation.

2. Implementing **strong ethical guidelines and oversight** for AI use in content creation and distribution.

3. Investing in **public education on digital literacy and critical thinking skills.**

4. Encouraging **collaboration** between tech companies, researchers, and policymakers **to address the challenges** posed by AI-generated misinformation."

My Conclusions About the AI Systems' Responses

- The concept that AI systems can reduce misinformation reminds me of one of my favorite sayings, "In theory it's all practical, but in practice it's all theoretical."[19]

- While good intentions, regulations, and the theoretical abilities of AI systems to reduce misinformation are all nice, the reality is that **bad actors** – or those operating in the gray zone of regulations – **will have the means and incentives to circumvent any guardrails created by governments or companies.**

---

19. See notes from the same quote at the beginning of this chapter.

- **It is very hard for people to detect AI-generated content.** As AI systems become more powerful and easy to use, AI-generated content (text, audio, video and images) will become more difficult for individuals to identify. That will continue because AI creators will be a step ahead of AI detectors in the ongoing "AI arms race."

Summary & Conclusions

- AI systems will likely look and function very differently in six months.

- Because we don't know yet whether governments will succeed in regulating the creation and use of AI systems,[20] it is very difficult to predict how AI will affect our information universe in the future.

- Even if governments put guardrails in place to minimize problems with the development and use of AI, rogue actors will still use AIs to create and spread misinformation. Some people have speculated that the future conflicts of superpowers will not involve bullets and bombs, but will be cyber-warfare waged or aided by AIs. That is all very worrisome.

- Only time will tell whether AI will reduce or increase misinformation, and how pervasively AI-generated misinformation will infect our society and cause harms.

---

20. https://www.nytimes.com/2023/06/14/technology/europe-ai-regulation.html, and https://www.brookings.edu/articles/the-eu-and-us-diverge-on-ai-regulation-a-transatlantic-comparison-and-steps-to-alignment/

- The future of our information world is unknown. Will it be dystopian or utopian? Will resistance be futile?[21] Or will HAL open the pod bay doors[22] so that virtual Rebel Alliance ships can attack the Emperor's death stars[23] of misinformation? Only time will tell.

- **Now, we can choose to be vaccinated and to vote, and to have productive conversations with people in real life.** In the future, if AI systems control certain aspects of our lives – or orchestrate a different social order or government structure – we may no longer have those choices. Only time will tell.

- As individuals, we can choose to take the red pill of enlightened reality, or the blue pill of stupefied existence, where we are controlled by AI systems.[24] We have the choice to be complacent about the world around us, or try to influence our friends, family and community when they are infected with AI-generated misinformation.

- As we create a future that includes Artificial Intelligence systems, only time will tell which path society will chose.

---

21. See the assimilation philosophy of the human-computer hybrid race Borg in the fictional series "Star Trek: The Next Generation." https://en.wikipedia.org/wiki/Borg

22. The sentient computer system in "2001: A Space Odyssey" refuses to open the space ship's outer doors to allow the reentry of the manned space pod. https://news.wjct.org/2023-07-31/open-the-pod-bay-door-hal-heres-how-ai-became-a-movie-villain and https://blog.shi.com/next-generation-infrastructure/open-the-pod-bay-doors-hal-whats-your-relationship-with-ai/

23. https://www.starwars.com/databank/death-star

24. https://www.britannica.com/topic/red-pill-and-blue-pill

A Few Final Words

Dear Readers,

Congratulations! You've made it through the entire book – assuming you didn't just flip to this page to see if it was a summary. In which case, please do read at least the first three chapters.

My goal for this book was to give you insights and actionable guidance about misinformation. It is not intended to be a comprehensive resource for all people who have misinformed friends, family, and co-workers. If you have any suggestions for improvements for an updated version – which I hope to have out in 2025 – please let me know. You can reach me at RevMisinfo@HealthPolCom.com.

• • •

This book does not explore opinions and beliefs. It focuses on misinformation about facts: things that can be shown to be correct or incorrect. **Opinions and beliefs – unlike facts – can be judged as morally right or wrong. Opinions and beliefs are not correct or incorrect.** Differing views about extremely important matters such as culturally-based conflicts, tax policy, and body autonomy can divide families and communities, and are outside the scope of this book.

• • •

Please use the contents of this book with empathy and kindness.

As we have seen in 2024, wherever there is information, misinformation can be generated and spread. Misinformation grows from mistrust, and it incites further mistrust. It can affect people's decisions about important things like health care, weather, disaster relief, and election results. Purveyors of misinformation use it to advance their political, personal, and business agendas.

The physical world feels like an increasingly scary place, with rising sea levels, more intense storms and geopolitical conflicts, while much of the virtual world is a swirling storm of verbal abuse and misinformation. The two worlds connect when information is warped into misinformation and drives real-world actions. This all seems very alarming, but I do have hope – hope that change can happen one person at a time, one community at a time.

> **This book does not provide medical, other clinical, or therapy advice. Everyone should have their own primary care clinician. If you need professional therapy for personal or interpersonal issues or situations, please seek that out.**

As mentioned in the Introduction, the footnotes are also located on the book's webpage: www.healthpolcom.com/reversing-misinformation-book-project-2024/, with clickable links where appropriate. The QR code below will take you to that page.

Acknowledgements

As in other parts of this book, names have been changed, abbreviated, or removed to protect privacy.

Great People Who Helped with Reviewing, Feedback, Editing, Cover Designer and Others Facets of Producing the Book

- A.B. • C.C. • E.O. • H.B. • J.B. • M.R. • S.C. • S.R.

High Level Supporters – Producer/Executive Producer Types

- B.M. • Beth B. • R.R. • Steven P.

Sponsors of All Sorts

- Ann L. • Art T. • C.S. • Daniel F. • Daniel S. • Ellen O.
- George A. • George O. • H.H. • Howard S. • Jason H.
- John D. • K.H. • Karen J. • Kathy C. • Laurie T. • Martin K.
- Noah B. • Pat L. • Ray J. • Steve F. • Steven G.

Supporters & Friends

- A.I. • Anne I. • B.C. • Ben S. • Bill H. • Brian A. • Cathy C.
- Cecilia H. • Charlie N. • Doug L. • Elizabeth C. • G.M. • G.S.

- Harold L. • J.B. • Jeffrey B. • John C. • John M. • John M.
- Joseph S. • Justin S. • K.G. • Kathy C. • Kristen J. • Laura C.
- Lee L. • M.S. • Marie V. • Melody H. • Natasha S. • Nick M.
- Peg W. • Peggy L. • Renee H. • Rich L. • S.L. • Steve M.

Others Who've Been Supportive in Ways They May Know – or Not!

- B.G. • D.C. • D.W. • Gizmo • K.H. • K.L. • K.M.
- Madison • M.C. • S.R. • S.S. • T.C. • T.O.

www.ingramcontent.com/pod-product-compliance
Lightning Source LLC
Jackson TN
JSHW060752080125
76749JS00002B/3